ANDREW G.
NELSON

Where Was God?

An NYPD first responder's search for answers
following the terror attack of Sept 11th, 2001

ANDREW G. NELSON

Where Was God?

Cover Design Copyright © 2018 by Huntzman Enterprises

Cover photo by Anne Bybee, Copyright © 2001 Used with permission

Published by Huntzman Enterprises

Huntzman Enterprises

First Edition: September 2018
Second Edition: September 2020

ISBN-10: 0-9987562-5-3
ISBN-13: 978-0-9987562-5-7

Printed in the United States of America
1 3 5 7 9 10 8 6 4 2

Other Titles by Andrew G. Nelson

DEDICATION

To my wife Nancy, without whose love, support and constant encouragement this book would not have been possible. Thank you for always believing in me.

For my friend and partner, retired NYPD Lieutenant Paul Murphy, whom I had the honor of standing shoulder to shoulder with on that fateful day and who earned his 'angel wings' on January 4th, 2018. Your wisdom, wit and friendship are sorely missed. *Fidelis Ad Mortem*, brother.

And to God, through whom all things are truly possible.

Romans 8:28

"Lord, take me where you want me to go. Let me meet who you want me to meet. Tell me what you want me to say and keep me out of your way." – Father Mychal Judge, OFM, FDNY Chaplain (*World Trade Center Victim #0001*)

"And we know that in all things God works for the good of those who love him, who have been called according to his purpose." – **Romans 8:28** (NIV)

INDEX

INTRODUCTION

"Where was God?"

The book you are reading has been over five years in the making. During that same span of time I have written seven full-length novels, two novellas, and two non-fiction works. These combined works number in the thousands of pages and close to a million words.

So why exactly has this book taken so long to write?

Well, as I found with my fictional novels, authors need to wait until the voices in their head talk to them. Here, I had the *idea* to write the book, but God hadn't given me the words. Every time I sat down at my computer, it felt like I had a case of writer's block. I would end up writing and then re-writing the outline. Then I would save it and turn my attention toward other projects.

Little did I know that it wasn't just *words* that I was waiting on.

The idea to write this story first came to me in March 2013. The previous night I had the wonderful opportunity to speak at a youth ministry meeting in Auburn, Illinois; a town close to where I live. Over the years I had done several similar speaking engagements which ran the gamut between civic events, church gatherings, school lectures, and memorials commemorating the attacks, but this event was a slight bit unusual, from how it all came about.

About a year prior, I was having fits over my wisdom teeth. My dentist, who understands I suffer from *dental-phobia*, and who knows equally that I still carry a firearm, has always been *deferential* to my low tolerance for dental pain. He decided to refer me to an oral surgeon in a neighboring city for determination.

That first referral didn't work out, so I bit the bullet and dealt with it for as long as I could. That lasted until December.

In the interim, my dentist located another surgeon who took my insurance and I visited him in January. He agreed that all four wisdom teeth needed to be extracted. A short time later, I sat in his chair as the anesthesia took hold. In an interesting twist, as I sat there alone waiting to go *under*, I was listening to music play. What should come on, as I began to slip into the twilight? The Guns & Roses' rendition of *Knocking on Heaven's Door*.

Who says God doesn't have a sense of humor?

A short time later the wisdom teeth were removed, as was the pain, and my loving wife had arranged yet another *speaking engagement* for me with the receptionist who, along with her husband, ran the youth ministry at the Auburn church.

I am one of those people who believe that God can move Heaven and Earth, as He wishes, for me, but for some strange reason He uses my wife as the booking agent.

This speech was like the previous ones, and at the conclusion I began accepting questions. Yet this time, the inevitable question: "*Where was God*?" seemed much more poignant when it came from this group of young Christian kids.

It is a question that I have been repeatedly asked regarding the terrorist attacks of September 11th, 2001. I have said that if I had a dollar for every time someone asked me about it, I would most likely not be writing this book, as I would be retired and living a life of luxury in *Bora Bora*. That I am typing away at this keyboard shows that God has other plans for me.

At the present moment I am situated somewhere in Central Illinois, looking out my window and watching snow fall. To be honest, Bora Bora sounds a whole lot better, but if there is one thing I have learned over the last half decade of my life, it is that God's plans take precedence over our desires.

As I have said, the question of where God was on September 11th is one I have been asked many times. Mostly it is asked by Christians, who are trying to understand why this, or any tragedy, may happen, but also on rare occasion by those seeking to minimize God and rebuke the faithful.

I realized that when the question is posed by the latter, it is done to dismiss religion and is often left unchecked. Sadly, those who try to respond are often vilified, ridiculed, or demeaned. It is a sad condemnation of who we have become as a society, not just in America, but around the world. Yet, I must confess that I find myself troubled for those people who look to dismiss God.

In writing this, I can only pray that if this book finds its way into their hands, it opens their hearts and minds toward a unique way of thinking.

This book will not be for everyone, but I did not write it for everyone. I am a firm believer that we are given certain gifts for a specific purpose. I feel that it is my job to write this story, but it is God's job to bring it to the audience that needs to read at the right time in their life.

Whether you agree or disagree, I sincerely hope that this book will inspire you to take a deeper look into the issue and not be dismissive because it doesn't fit with the way you see things.

Each of us is on our own journey. This is *my story* of faith and coming to terms with the attack of September 11th as a first responder.

Andrew G. Nelson
Sergeant - NYPD (Retired)

CHAPTER ONE

(My Story)

Every story has a beginning, and mine does as well.

I think it is important to share this with you because I have always been skeptical of people who talk about something, but have no actual world experience. To me, it's like getting marriage counseling from someone who has never married; or the pep talk from someone who has never gone through a trial or tribulation in their life. My thoughts and feelings are not founded on some abstract theory, arrived at in the halls of academia, but on life experiences garnered in the real-world.

I was born and raised in the Richmond Hill section of Queens. Queens is one of the five boroughs, otherwise known as counties, which make up what is collectively known as New York City.

From an early age, I knew that I wanted to be a New York City Police Officer. My late grandfather, James Maguire, was an old school, first-generation Irish-American, Catholic, Truck Driver. He'd wanted to be a cop, but he wasn't able to pass the medical background they had back in his day. We're talking the old days of iron men and wooden nightsticks. He had the pedigree for the job; he just didn't have the height to meet the strict physical requirements at that time.

However, his job as a truck driver brought him into contact with a lot of cops and being the Irishman that he was, he forged friendships with them that lasted throughout his lifetime. Back in the early seventies, when the city was going to *hell in a handbasket*, a lot of those cops were getting laid off. My grandfather was able to get them jobs, working for the trucking company that he was now a foreman for, and they never forgot him for what he did.

I remember as a young kid being in my grandparent's apartment in Richmond Hill. The doorbell would ring and the next

4

thing I knew there would be two cops coming in. Occasionally I'd be handed their black leather jackets and hats to go lay on the bed while they talked and had a *cold one*. Things were much different back then.

I'd lay them down reverently, mesmerized by the shiny chrome shields and medals that adorned their jackets. What can I say? While some kids grow up idolizing athletes and musicians, my heroes were cops.

How buffy was I?

I can tell you I was the only kid attending St. Benedict Joseph Labre Elementary School that had a PDNY tie bar. I can also tell you I still have that tie bar to this day.

Back then, we grew up in what I considered a close knit community. That is every parent *knew you*. If your mother needed you she leaned out the window and called your name. The *Mother Telegraph Service* would then repeat the message until you acknowledged back. The *technology* might have been crude, but to be honest it worked much better than cell phones.

To the best of my knowledge, everyone's parent had a first name, but there was no way on God's little green earth that we would ever have had the audacity to acknowledge it. They were either Mr. or Mrs. and we were fine with that.

I attended Catholic elementary school back when we had nuns who wore habits. Stories abound about the ruthlessness of nuns and their ability to wield a ruler or pointer. I am here to confirm that those outrageous, wild, and colorful tales are 100% true. My knuckles still ache on wintry days, but I was what you would call a good Roman Catholic boy. I was baptized, took first communion, and had my confirmation; all replete with the traditional pomp and circumstance that accompanies such milestone events.

I spent eight glorious years attending *St. Bennies* with many of those years serving as an altar boy. This would provide much comedic relief to those who knew me later in life. What

Catholic school didn't teach me was how to adapt to a public high school. That I had to learn on my own and it was a helluva learning curve.

Unfortunately, I was not a dutiful student. Not that I didn't have the ability, far from it, I was just bored. By my senior year I had screwed up and cut school enough times to be held over. It seemed that I had managed to get myself into the *super-senior* category and was now working on the four and a half year high school degree program. So I dropped out. Later in life I would officially state that I had *"voluntarily dis-enrolled."*

At the time, school wasn't much of a concern; I had money in my pocket and dreams in my head. I had already gotten my first *real job* when I was fifteen, working as a security guard for an agency run by a former New York City cop. I might have been too young, but I was over six feet tall and smoked. So I didn't get too many questions. I worked in Manhattan and commuted in on the weekends, working the 4x12 shift at an upscale location around the corner from Grand Central Station.

After a while the commuting got to me and I got a local job working with some friends at a grocery store. It may sound strange, but I have the fondest memories of working there. I worked with some exceptional people and had a blast. Now, thirty-plus years later, I often wish I could go back for a day and relive those moments.

If you're reading this, and you're thinking, 'God, I'm stuck in a thankless job,' fear not. You're there for a reason. It might be to learn more about yourself or to appreciate something or someone. That doesn't mean that you will understand that *today*, but one day it will all make sense. You just have to trust in God.

When I was 16 ½, I was eligible to file to take the NYPD exam. Back then you had to pay to take the test and the competition was fierce. They held the testing in schools throughout NYC, and I recall standing in this enormous line that seemed to snake around the school. At the time I wondered if I was just wasting my Saturday with all of the people I was going up

6

against. To my shock, I did well enough to get a spot on the list, but I was too young to get appointed. When they passed my number over, I knew that it was just a matter of waiting until I was of age. That was the hardest part of all. I can't think of too many teenagers who are good at waiting.

After what would have been my senior year of high school, my parents split up and eventually got divorced. My mother took me and my two brothers to Rockaway Beach, which had once been known as the *Irish Riviera*.

Rockaway is a peninsula in the southern part of Queens. At its western border is Breezy Point, a neighborhood that was decimated during Super Storm Sandy in 2012, and at its eastern edge is Far Rockaway, which links the peninsula with Long Island. What had once been New York City's Playground, and a respite for the large Irish population of the early to mid-1900s, soon fell into economic despair.

The Co-op that we lived in was one of many that dotted the shoreline facing the Atlantic Ocean, and directly behind our Co-op was a series of New York City Housing Authority apartment buildings.

Back in the 1950s, in an effort at urban renewal, the City of New York constructed new residential buildings. What had started off as affordable, middle income apartments soon turned into low income and subsidized housing. It wasn't long before the vast majority of the middle-income families fled. The subsequent void was filled by a criminal element that preyed on residents as well as those in the surrounding area. Within the first six months we were there, my mother's car was stolen and someone mugged both my brothers on their way home from school. What had once been an Irish mecca, had since become just another tough New York City neighborhood.

It was during that time that I had seen an advertisement for the New York City Police Department Auxiliary program. I thought it would be an excellent idea to join and get a glimpse into what police work was like while I waited to get called to go into the police academy. After what happened to my brothers, I thought it might be a way to make a positive impact.

I joined the 100th Precinct Auxiliary in late 1983 and was soon out patrolling the streets. It didn't take long to figure out that some of the locals didn't have any use for *unarmed volunteers* and the real cops looked at us like we were *certifiable idiots*. Back then, being a NYC cop was tough and it was a harsh introduction to law enforcement.

Today the death of a NYC police officer, from other than 9/11 related illnesses, is rare thank God, but when I came on, I remember going to funerals on a regular basis. In fact, in my first five years of being a police officer we had twenty-five line-of-duty deaths in just sixty months; an average of roughly one every two-and-a-half months.

However, my choice to join the auxiliary program would have a far reaching impact. During the training process I met up with a guy who was also from my test. He had a higher number than I had and yet he was already being processed. He gave me the name of his investigator and I reached out to them to see what was happening. I was told that they had already tried to contact me several times, but they returned all the letters as undeliverable.

Remember that divorce?

Someone neglected to tell me about this thing called a *forwarding address* card for the postal service. It seemed as if my police career was doomed even before it began.

I called out to my grandfather to see if he knew anyone who could help me. As luck would have it, he knew a cop that used to work at the 103rd Precinct who was now an investigator in the applicant processing division. He reached out to him and that began a whirlwind investigation. There were a series of medical exams, psychological exams, interviews, etc. Everything was happening at a break-neck speed, until a minor blip popped up on the investigative radar.

Looking back now, especially considering how they have relaxed the entry requirements, it seems absurd that my law enforcement career was almost derailed by a summons which I had gotten two years earlier, but it was.

After moving to Rockaway, I had continued to work at the supermarket in my old neighborhood. As a result, I had to take two trains and walk about a mile to get there. One evening, in the middle of winter, I was stuck at the Broad Channel station waiting for the train. It was freezing and somewhere around midnight.

Waiting for the train at this time of night was an exercise in futility. Working late meant that I didn't get into the station until after the normal operating schedule was over, so it seemed as if the train came and went sporadically. I needed a cigarette, so I left the comfort of the heated train station and walked to the *far end* of the outside platform.

I thought there was no one else at that station except for me and the bored looking token clerk, but, much to my chagrin, a New York City Transit cop began walking toward me, just as I was finishing my cigarette. He Proceeded to write me a summons for smoking within a transit facility.

It took me a while to locate the receipt for the money order I had used to pay the summons, but I eventually did and was able to get it all squared away. The entire applicant process, which should have taken upward of a year or more, took only a handful of months and in December 1984 I was notified that I was to be sworn in as a police officer in the January 1985 academy class.

My academy class was so large that they needed to hold the paper-work and swearing in at a college campus in Queens. We were over 2,000 strong.

Back then we worked alternating 8x4 or 4x12 shifts and we rotated days off. After a while I enjoyed the Saturday and Sunday shifts, because the commute was much easier. The academy was in Manhattan and I had to travel by train every day. I soon learned that one of my classmates lived in East New York and he drove in. I would catch a lift with him in the evenings and that cut out much of my train ride.

Because we had so many recruits in our academy, some of us went to the range earlier on. I mentioned that I went into the academy in January, right? Going to the range in February was all sorts of *special*. My class actually qualified in what could only be described as a *blizzard*. We would have complained, but the instructors were kind enough to point out that gunfights do not take place only on bright sunny days. On July 2nd, 1985, my academy class proudly walked out of Madison Square Garden as the newest members of the New York City Police Department.

I have to admit that after leaving elementary school, my interest in religion waned. I no longer attended church, save for the obligatory holidays of Christmas and Easter or when required by a wedding or funeral. My new job also didn't help. It is very hard to see man's inhumanity to man played out every shift. Don't get me wrong, I still believed in God, but there was no relationship.

I got married in November 1985. In life there are always defining moments when you either listen or you don't. In retrospect, this was one of those moments where I forged ahead, even when I knew it was a mistake.

When a marriage works, two people grow together, but when it doesn't, they grow apart. It seems like a simple enough concept, yet everywhere we look we watch the rise in the divorce rate and seem perplexed by the issue. I've concluded that the reason we have these issues is that we have taken God out of the equation.

My thoughts on this come from my Christian belief, but I also include Judaism, as the basic tenant I cite comes from the Old Testament. In **Genesis 2** it is written, "*And the rib, which the Lord God had taken from man, made he a woman, and brought her unto the man. And Adam said, 'This is now bone of my bones, and flesh of my flesh: she shall be called Woman, because she was taken out of Man.' Therefore shall a man leave his father and his mother, and shall cleave unto his wife: and they shall be one flesh.*" (KJV)

If the union of marriage is ordained by God, then why do marriages fail? The answer I believe is that we as human beings have decided that we will do things on our own, without God's input. So instead of seeking Godly spouses, we seek worldly ones, those who are attractive, affluent, or ones who closely associate to our values or interests. When the marriage fails, we take the worldly way out. In this day and age, everything is disposable.

In getting married, I thought I was doing what was *right*. I now had a career and a spouse. In a few years I had a son, followed by a house on Long Island, and a few years later a daughter. I had also been promoted to detective and was working in the NYPD's elite Intelligence Division doing dignitary protection.

You would think I had it all. To my friends and family I did, but the reality was that I was miserable. I could sit here and point out where each of us failed, but it's not my place. When you are honest in self-reflection you focus not on others, but on yourself. I failed in many areas, but the biggest failure was that during my life I had allowed my relationship with God to falter.

In 1997, everything fell apart, but the old saying that, "*if God closes one door, He opens another*," was about to come true for me.

I had just been promoted to sergeant and I was transferred out of the Intelligence Division. As a new sergeant, I expected to work the New Year's Eve detail, but as fate would have it my new assignment schedule, as a city-wide supervisor, had me off. As a result, I ended up meeting my wife Nancy in the *new, old fashioned way*. That is to say we met on-line before it was the *in-thing* to do.

Back then, *chatting* was not the socially acceptable medium that it is today. Still, it provided a fresh group of friends who I could be open with and knew they would not judge me. I'd say that chatting caused me to disconnect further, but the truth was I had already done that. You know when you have given up and I had.

Nancy was safe, largely in part because she lived a thousand miles away in Illinois. She was interesting, funny, and willing to listen to me vent. She was going through a similar issue on her side; so we became each other's cheering squad, and each other's shoulder to cry on. What started out as an innocent friendship had grown into something much more.

In the interim, I had moved out and rented a place in Central Islip. The toughest thing for me was being away from my kids. I had been there from the moment they were born and they were everything to me. In fact, they were the only reason I had stayed as long as I did. I wasn't the perfect dad, but I was a devoted one.

During this time Nancy had gotten divorced and I had traveled several times out to Illinois to see her. It didn't take long for us to realize that we were in love with each other. Between the travel costs and the phone bills, we decided that we had to come to a better arrangement. I still had a half dozen more years to do before I could retire from the police department. So Nancy packed up her two boys and made the thousand mile trek to Long Island, where we had rented a house in the North Bellmore section of Nassau County. In May 1999, my divorce was official and Nancy and I got married.

I'd like to say things were perfect, but they weren't. It is tough blending families, but we did the best that we could. Sadly, there was a lot of pressure from my family pertaining to my children and financial issues. While most it was flat-out wrong, it did cause a lot of emotional stress for Nancy and I.

It was during this time that something remarkable happened. One day Nancy and I had been talking about religion. She knew that I was a non-practicing Catholic, and I knew that she was a born-again Christian. It was an interesting conversation that forced me to re-think my prior belief structure.

I had always had an *issue* with the Catholic Church. Particularly since what I was *told* rarely sounded like the same thing I had *read* in the Bible. One specific point for me was

Purgatory, that *in-between place* where you wait until you are *free enough* from sin to pass on into heaven.

I want to note something here before I continue. Please understand that I do not undertake to attack or undermine anyone's personal views on religion. The thoughts I express here are *my own* and have come about through a lot of unique experiences, examination, and introspection. If anything I write makes you think deeper than I feel that it is God's will. I believe that we all have an obligation to share *our* faith with others, but then God does the rest by working in that person's heart and mind. Sometimes that takes the form of a simple question or statement that causes us to examine things closer.

I soon took a more critical theological look into things and reviewed my entire belief structure. I realized that I believed in the tenants of *Sola Gratia, Sola Fide, and Sola Scriptura;* which is the belief that the Bible (*Scriptura*) is the supreme source of authority for the church and that we have salvation by Grace (*Gratia*) through Faith (*Fide*) alone. Or as Paul says in **Ephesians 2:8**, *"For it is by grace you have been saved, through faith, and this is not from yourselves, it is the gift of God."* (NIV)

It was also during this time that I lost my father, which came as a terrible blow. We had always had a tumultuous relationship as I was growing up and we had not spoken in several years. One day I was at work and I got a call that he was in the hospital and was extremely sick. I was told that the prognosis was not good and I needed to get there right away.

I left work early, drove home, and picked up Nancy. The two of us headed upstate to the hospital, which was located near Albany. When I got there, he was in a small room in a semi-coma and each member of my family spent some private time with him.

In all honesty, I had feared him as a boy, but now he seemed different. At that moment he was not the man I had grown up loathing. He seemed almost fragile, lying on the hospital bed, and instinctively I knew he would be gone soon. I reached down and took his hand in my own. It was cold and slightly stiff. I gripped it, as if trying to will some of the warmth from my own hands to pass into his.

When you face the realization that life is ending for the person in front of you, the finality causes you to question what things are important. As I held his hand I told him I loved him and that I was sorry for the years that had passed between us. I told him I knew he loved me in his own way and that at the time it was the best that he could. I also told him he was dying and that there was no way to stop that.

Then I did something that in months earlier I would not have had the ability to do. I *preached* to my father the gospel of salvation. I explained that the only way into Heaven was through accepting Jesus Christ as his Lord and savior. That it was a gift from God, something he only had to accept. I then kissed him on his forehead, told him again that I loved him, and that it was okay to let go.

In that moment, I felt something that has always stayed with me and always will. I felt the slightest bit of pressure against my hand.

In my heart, I believe that he was letting me know he heard and understood what I had shared with him.

Nancy and I returned home that night and made plans to head back up early in the morning. I had just sat down on the edge of the bed when my cell phone rang. I answered it and the woman on the line asked if I was Andrew Nelson and I said I was. She told me she was a nurse at the hospital and explained that she had tried to get hold of both his wife and my mother, but there was no answer. She was sorry to have to tell me that my father had passed away.

I thanked her for letting me know, and then I thanked God for giving me that opportunity to have one last conversation with my dad before he died.

Was he a Christian? I don't know. Did he accept Christ? I don't know that either, but one day I will.

What I have learned in my life was that God works in very mysterious ways. We can spend our life in rebellion, acting and working outside of His will for us, and we can make an utter mess of things. But it is during times like this, when we least expect it, that He brings people or events into our lives to teach us something, and then it is our job to reach out to others.

It is a lesson I would come to know all too well on the morning of September 11th, 2001.

CHAPTER TWO

(September 11th, 2001)

Anyone can tell you where they were, and what they were doing, on the morning of September 11th, 2001.

That moment has been forever seared into our national psyche. I imagine it is the same for most tragic events. If you were alive on December 7th, 1941, I am sure you recall where you were when you first heard the reports about the bombing of Pearl Harbor. Likewise, where you were on November 22nd, 1963, when you heard that President John F. Kennedy had been assassinated. Fortunately, these moments are rare, but when they occur they merge us together, from the disparate people that we normally are, into a collective group known simply as: *Americans*. We lay aside all disagreements for a moment in time; as we bond together during times of national tragedy.

For those who were in New York City that day, most will recall how clear the sky was. It was one of those rare, cool late summer days where the sun shined bright and the sky was a crystal blue without a cloud in the sky. It was what pilots refer to as *severe clear*, a sky so clear that there is seemingly infinite visibility.

But this weather condition would only serve to make the scene that was about to unfold even more surreal.

The morning of September 11th, 2001, I was a sergeant working in the Chief of Patrol's Investigation and Evaluation Section. My unit was the investigative arm for the Chief, but we also served as a city-wide monitoring unit for major events. One of these functions was to supervise election posts throughout the city and make sure there were no issues. September 11th was the primary election day in New York City. Election monitoring was always an early day for us because voting locations began opening at 6 a.m. in the city.

I met my driver, Police Officer Ramon Otero, over at Highway Patrol Unit #3 on the Grand Central Parkway in Queens. I had a *category two* vehicle assigned to me, which meant I could use it anywhere while I was working, but had to park it at a police facility, within the city limits, at the end of my shift. We met a little before our shift began and made our way toward Brooklyn.

Election monitoring was a fairly mundane assignment. I would check to make sure there were no issues with either the polling booths or the personnel. Then I would locate the officer assigned to the location and I would sign their memo books to document I had visited them.

As a general rule, when working a day shift, I kept the department radio in my car tuned to the Traffic Division frequency. Since we were a city-wide unit, and this was New York City, it was always good to know where the traffic delays were. We often joked that, while most places had a rush hour, New York City had rush *hours and hours*.

At around 8:45 a.m. we were just pulling up in front of a school, in the Canarsie section, when I heard a call for an *explosion* come over the radio from one of the police officers assigned to a traffic post at the World Trade Center.

In the past, when I have shared my story, it often amazes people that this did not cause me any genuine concern. It has been my experience that explosions happen in New York City all the time and they come in all shapes and sizes. It is common to hear about manhole covers blowing, along with water heaters, steam pipes, etc. The officer's voice seemed quite calm to me, and my only thought was that it would screw up traffic around the area.

I made my way into the school gym and located the assigned officer. We spoke for a few moments about what was going on and I signed her memo book. Little did I know that it would be the last memo book I would sign that day.

I got back into the car and I made an entry in the log sheet we kept; showing the location and the time that I visited. We had just

17

pulled away from the curb when another call came over the radio stating that a plane had struck one of the towers.

Now, here comes the amazing part. This didn't strike me as odd either. When I was in the Intelligence Division, besides the investigative role we performed, we also provided dignitary protection. In my five years with the Division I worked on many security details including Pope Saint John Paul II, former President's William Clinton, George H. W. Bush, and Jimmy Carter, along with numerous foreign dignitaries. As a result, I spent many hours, during these high profile visits, providing aerial reconnaissance over the city with the Aviation Unit. What I learned was that the area over the Hudson and East Rivers, the two bodies of water that flank either side of the island of Manhattan, is referred to as *unrestricted airspace*.

What this meant was that aircraft flying along these routes did not have to report to any of the three major air traffic control towers at John F. Kennedy, LaGuardia, and Newark airports. So on any given day, especially a clear one, you would have small, fixed wing planes and helicopters ferrying business executives or sightseers around Manhattan, especially down to the Statue of Liberty.

This area was well known for the volume of air traffic and there were several heliports along the waterfront. When I flew with the Aviation Unit, anytime I wasn't watching the motorcade below, my head was on a swivel trying to spot in-bound aircraft.

You would think it would have change after September 11th, but you'd be wrong.

In October 2006, N.Y. Yankee baseball pitcher, Cory Lidle, was flying north, along the East River, when his plane crashed into a 40-story condominium tower on Manhattan's Upper East Side. The crash killed both Lidle and his pilot-instructor. Then, in August 2009, a plane and helicopter crashed over the Hudson River, sparking renewed calls for restrictions. Some older New Yorker's might even recall that in July 1945, a military B-25 bomber struck the Empire State Building in poor weather conditions.

The bottom line is that a plane crashing into the Towers, while tragic, was not unthinkable.

I called my wife on my cellphone to let her know what was going on. At the time she was working for a manufacturing company that made parts for the airline industry. They didn't have a television set, so she turned on the local radio station to see if they were covering it.

In the meantime, Ramon and I headed over to the Dunkin' Donut's on Rockaway Parkway and pulled into the parking lot. I remember that I was standing in line when Ramon came rushing in. Immediately, I could tell from the look on his face that something wasn't right. He called for me to come out and he had my cellphone in his hand. It was my wife.

Nancy told me she had been listening to the *Bob and Tom Show* on the radio and they were watching the live video feed coming into their studio. As they were describing what was going on, they witnessed a second plane strike the South Tower.

It was just after 9:00 a.m.

At the time I remember thinking that I don't believe in coincidences and that this was no longer just a tragedy. I switched the radio from the Traffic Division to the Special Operations Division.

S.O.D. is the parent command for the Emergency Service Unit. ESU is referred to as the New York City Police Department's version of SWAT, but they are much more diverse than that. They have their roots in handling all types of rescues, from bridge jumpers to building collapses. They are the department's *Jack of All Trades*.

Besides ESU, Aviation is also on that frequency, and I monitored the radio to hear what was being reported. Ramon wanted to head directly in to Manhattan, but I recall feeling very uneasy; something wasn't sitting right with me.

As I mentioned earlier, I had spent five years planning and conducting security for high profile dignitary visits while assigned to the Intelligence Division. The risk of a terror attack was always something we had to consider.

As street cops, we had been trained to *keep looking*. This meant that if you found one suspect, you looked for an accomplice. If you were searching a perp and found a weapon, you kept searching to see if there was another. This same mentality held true for protection. There is a general rule that stipulates: No matter how positive you are, that there isn't another attack or explosive device, you *always* assume there is.

There is an excellent reason for this *mantra*. Terrorists realized that they were missing out on an opportunity to inflict even greater casualties and cause more fear. So they adjusted their tactics. They designed the initial attack to draw in the first responders, military, police, fire, and medical personnel, and then they would launch a second, more devastating attack. The message was simple and effective: *If they can't protect themselves, how can they protect you*?

So my immediate thought was: *With everyone's focus on the fiery inferno raging above them, would anyone even notice all of the trucks and cars around them*?

My mind was filled with images of car bombs going off.

People have a tendency to believe that September 11th was the first terror attack in New York, but that's not true. The city has had a significant history of attacks over the last hundred years.

- On September 16th, 1920, there was a bombing on Wall Street which left thirty-eight people dead and wounded another three hundred.

- On July 4th, 1940, a bomb at the British Pavilion in the World's Fair exploded, killing two NYC Police Officers.

- From 1940 through 1956, the *Mad Bomber,* George Metesky, placed over thirty bombs throughout the city, wounding ten people.

- In 1960, the *Sunday Bomber* set off a series of bombs on subways and ferries during Sundays and Holidays, killing one and injuring fifty others.

- From August through November 1969, *The Weather Underground* set off bombs at the Marine Midland Building, Federal Building, Armed Forces Induction Center, and the Manhattan Criminal Court, wounding numerous people.

- On May 21, 1971, the Black Liberation Army assassinated NYC Police Officer's Waverly Jones and Joseph Piagentini.

- On January 27, 1972, the Black Liberation Army assassinated NYC Police Officer's Rocco Laurie and Gregory Foster.

- In December 1972, a Cuban exile group bombed a travel agency in Queens.

- On March 4, 1973, *Black September*, a Palestinian militant group attempted a car bombing during a visit by Israeli Prime Minister Golda Meir.

- On December 11th, 1974, a bomb set off by the *FALN*, a Puerto Rican militant group, exploded and severely wounded a NYC Police Officer.

- On January 24th, 1975, a bomb set off by the *FALN* explodes at the historic Fraunces Tavern, killing four and wounding over fifty others.

- On April 19th, 1975, the *FALN* set off four bombs in Manhattan, injuring five people.

- On December 29th, 1975, a bomb exploded at LaGuardia Airport, killing eleven people and injuring seventy-five others.

- On September 10th – 11th, 1976, NYC Police Officer Brian Murray was killed, and several wounded, while trying to defuse a bomb in a locker left by Croatian freedom fighters who had hijacked a plane.

- On August 3rd, 1977, the *FALN* set off a bomb at the Mobil HQ, killing one and injuring eight other people. Five days later another bomb was located at the American Express building.

- On June 3rd, 1980, a bomb was detonated at the Statue of Liberty story room.

- On February 26, 1993, the First World Trade Center bombing killed six and injured over a thousand.

- On February 24, 1997, a Palestinian opened fire on tourists at the observation deck atop the Empire State Building, killing one and wounding several others.

- On October 8, 2000, Molotov cocktails were thrown at a synagogue on the eve of Yom Kippur in the Bronx.

Since September 11th, 2001, there have been many other terror attacks, including the assassination of NYC Police Officer's Rafael Ramos and Wenjian Liu along with the attempted murder of two other officers. These attacks have resulted in more than a dozen deaths and dozens more injured.

So the belief that a terror attack was underway, in the heart of the Big Apple, was at the forefront of my thoughts, as we were driving west on the Belt Parkway, toward Manhattan.

My protection training was screaming inside my head, like a warning claxon on a Navy ship, telling me to *slow down* and proceed with caution.

I told Ramon to get off at the Flatbush Avenue exit and go to the Special Operations Division. At that time, the radio transmissions were chaotic. I wanted to see if I could get a coherent update as to what was happening at the scene, and to see if there was any coordinated response that was being started.

We arrived at S.O.D. and went to the Investigations Unit. For me, it was the first opportunity to see what had happened. On the old TV set I watched as the news played the feed from the scene. Thick black smoke was billowing from the massive gashes carved out by the two planes. I watched as people hung in the open spaces, clinging to the ragged metal façade, of what had only minutes earlier been offices.

I couldn't imagine what was going through their minds. To be torn between the fires that raged behind them and the abyss that stood before them is beyond my comprehension. As I watched the television screen in front of me, I saw someone make that ultimate choice and jump.

I felt sick then, and I still do to this day.

All around me it felt as if I was in a sea of pandemonium and I was struggling to make sense out of the chaos.

No one had any clue about what was going on or where we should go. There was talk of boarding buses and heading off to a staging area in another part of Brooklyn. I decided we would not go sit on our hands and wait for someone to make a decision. We got back in the car and made our way north on Flatbush Avenue, heading back toward the Belt Parkway. I didn't know what we could do, considering the magnitude of what I had just witnessed on the TV, but we were going in.

A week earlier I had given up smoking cold-turkey and spent the last several days walking around chewing on coffee stirrers. Even though I had successfully *kicked the habit*, as we drove up Flatbush Avenue I realized that there was no way that I would make it through the day without a cigarette.

I called Nancy to let her know what was going on and to inform her I was officially *un-quitting* smoking. I told her we going to Manhattan and that I would try to let her know what was going on when we got there. I could hear the panic in her voice.

I don't recall the exact conversation we had, but it went something like this:

"I just wanted to let you know we are heading in."

"You can't go in; you don't even have your [bullet resistant] vest with you."

"Nancy, they're flying planes into buildings, I don't think my vest is going to help me."

"You don't have to go; they don't even know you're out there."

"I have to go."

"I can't believe you are putting your job over your family. What about us? We need you."

"Honey, I'm a cop. It's what I do."

"Please don't go."

"I have to. I love you. I will call you and let you know what is going on as soon as I can."

In retrospect, it's painful for me to relive that and yet I cannot fathom what was going through her mind at that moment. Nancy and I had only been married for just over two years. She had moved herself and her two boys one thousand miles away from her family to be with me. There was no one here for her to turn to, no one to comfort her, as she sat by the phone and waited.

New York might be known as the *big melting pot*, but it is not necessarily a friendly one. I liken it more to a crucible where you are either vanquished or forged into something much stronger through adversity. At that moment I could re-direct my focus toward my job, but what did she have to turn to? She was alone.

In so many ways it speaks to the incredible sacrifice that the spouses and children of our police, fire, and military personnel go through every day. They send their loved one's into harm's way, knowing that they might never come back through the door. They are truly the unsung heroes and there is no way to re-pay them for the sacrifices they make every day.

As Nancy sat in her office, forty miles away, we continued up Flatbush Avenue. I told Ramon to take me to a store to get cigarettes. We stopped at the corner of Avenue U where there was a small tobacco shop. I walked in and everyone, including the counter-man, was quietly staring up at the television screen. I asked the man for a pack of Marlboro Ultra-Light 100's and watched as he turned around to grab a pack, but the slot was empty. He turned back with a confused look on his face, as he informed me that they were out.

For a moment we just stared at one another. The idea that they were out of Marlboro's second most popular brand of cigarettes seemed ludicrous, and yet the empty slot told the story.

I honestly have no idea why I didn't just select another brand, but I just turned around and walked back out to the car. As I got in, Ramon asked if we were ready and I told him no. I explained that they didn't have my brand, but I knew there was a gas station nearby, so I told him to take me over there. Again I encountered the same bewildered looking people, but I was able to get my cigarettes and headed back outside. I remember lighting up even before I made it to the car door.

We headed south on Flatbush Ave and got on the westbound Belt Parkway, driving toward Manhattan. From the moment we got on the parkway we were caught up in bumper to bumper traffic. Even with lights and siren blaring, it was a tough go. This section of the Belt Parkway crossed a nearby bridge, with the Atlantic Ocean on the left and Shell Bank Creek on the right. So there weren't many options for the vehicles in front of us to move over. As we continued through traffic, Ramon attempted to traverse the roadway when possible on the shoulders.

I just thought it was the tail end of the morning rush hour, but I soon realized that people had abandoned their vehicles and were standing outside. The portion of the Belt Parkway that we were on at the time was in a low-lying marsh area. This particular stretch of roadway provided an unobstructed view of the distant Manhattan skyline.

I don't think there is any way you can prepare to *see* something like that with your own eyes. As I said, the sky was the most amazing color blue which created the perfect contrast for the skyscrapers that rose up in the distance, the sun glinting off their façades of metal and glass. In the center stood the two massive structures known to all as the *Twin Towers*, black smoke continuing to pour out of them. As we continued to make our way toward Manhattan all I could think about was how do you even *respond* to something like that?

As we were driving in, I received another call from Nancy. She informed me they were now reporting that the Pentagon, in Arlington, Virginia, had also been hit. At this point I could no longer deny the obvious and I said, "*We're being attacked.*"

Nancy was confused and was crying. She asked, "*By who?*" Unfortunately, I didn't have an answer for her. For as long as I could remember we have always had an extensive list of countries who didn't like us for a variety of reasons. These ranged from financial to religious and just about anything and everything in between.

I told her I loved her and hung up the phone. It was all a bit overwhelming, as I tried to process the information.

Are there more? I wondered.

While Ramon continued to navigate the car through the congestion, I focused on listening to the radio. Confusion, panic, and calm were all being thrown into the mix. One moment you would hear frantic calls to send more help, the next you would hear supervisors announcing staging areas for responding units to report to, followed by an on-scene unit cautioning others that bodies were falling from the towers.

One particular radio transmission from the Aviation Unit stood out in my mind. After the first World Trade Center attack in 1993, they put evacuation protocols in place that directed certain occupants of the South Tower to proceed to the observation deck where a helicopter landing platform was located. The only problem was that the helicopters could not land there on September 11th, because of the amount of smoke billowing upward obscured the rooftop helipad.

As I listened, the pilot was telling the radio dispatcher to get word to Port Authority to tell the people not to go to the helipad because they couldn't land. You could hear the despair in the voice. There were several helicopters in the air when the South Tower went down. I imagine that this image still haunts those pilots and crew members.

We continued to fight the traffic as we made our way west. When we had reached the Verrazano Narrows Bridge, we had an unobstructed view of lower Manhattan.

I can't recall what was going through our minds at that very moment time. I don't remember talking during the entire trip. I guess that each of us was mentally trying to come to terms with what lay ahead. The image that now confronted us was a visual assault on the senses and left no doubt as to what we were responding to. Thick, black smoke blocked our view and cast an eerie pall over the skyline.

In my career I have pursued armed suspects, rushed burning houses, and put my life in harm's way more times than I ever want to think about, but at those times you are not thinking about the risks. Most of the time you don't see the danger until you are right in the middle of it, but this was different.

The trip thus far had seemed to be agonizingly slow. With each passing minute we could hear the tragedy unfolding on the radio, but now, as I looked at the horrifying image in front of me, I was not sure if we would live to see September 12th. At one point I recall turning to Ramon and said something to the effect of: "*I don't know what is going to happen today, but it was an honor working with you.*"

Sadly, we only *thought* we knew what we were heading in to, but it was about to get so much worse.

It was not until we got on the Gowanus Expressway that we could race ahead. The Highway Patrol had gotten a blocker car positioned in the roadway and shut down any civilian traffic into Manhattan. As our car sped ahead unobstructed, we covered the entire length of the highway in a matter of seconds.

The Gowanus Expressway ends at the entrance to the Brooklyn Battery Tunnel; which travels under the East River and exits out into lower Manhattan. One lane of the tunnel exits onto Greenwich Street and the other onto West Street, about three blocks from the South Tower.

As we approached the toll plaza, I could see a fire truck sitting in the roadway. I hadn't given it much thought until a fireman jumped from the rig and stood in our way. Ramon brought the car to a stop and I was just about to scream something unpleasant out of the passenger window at him when the unbelievable happened.

Directly behind the fireman, I watched as an explosion of thick, gray smoke erupted from the mouth of the tunnel.

To understand the scope of what we were witnessing, you have to know the physical makeup of the Brooklyn Battery Tunnel. It comprises two individual tubes, one heading into Manhattan while the other heads into Brooklyn. Each tube has two lanes and they are massive. I'm not sure of the exact dimensions, but I feel confident in saying that they are each well over a dozen feet high by about twenty feet wide.

When I have tried to explain the image we encountered, I have told people to visualize taking a drag on a cigarette and then expelling it through a straw. That same force of smoke was what we witnessed coming from the mouth of the tunnel.

My initial thought was that my worst fears were coming true. That we had just witnessed a secondary attack and that they had blown up the tunnel.

As I watched, I saw people begin to emerge; gray people. I could tell from their build that they were either men or women, but that was about it. From head to toe they were covered in gray soot and they had an almost extraterrestrial appearance.

It was as if my brain was being visually assaulted and my mind struggled to process the image. What we didn't know was that 2 World Trade Center (the South Tower) had just fallen and that smoke and ash was the remnants of the collapse of the 110 story building.

Just to give you an idea of the force necessary to send the debris shooting out the tunnel, consider that the tunnel is 9,117 feet long and is the longest continuous underwater vehicular tunnel in North America.

The Brooklyn Battery Tunnel fell under the jurisdiction of the Triborough Bridge and Tunnel Authority, who were already on-scene along with the aforementioned FDNY personnel. In my mind, the primary response location was still the Towers, so I told Ramon to back up and we made our way off the highway via an entrance ramp, then proceeded north up Hicks Street. I had worked in this area before, so I knew that Hicks would lead us up to Atlantic Avenue. From there we could get onto the Brooklyn Queens Expressway and make our way over the Brooklyn Bridge into Manhattan. As we headed up to the bridge, I glanced out the driver's side window and saw the entire lower Manhattan skyline blocked out by thick smoke.

I'm not sure why, but I have no recollection of getting onto the Brooklyn Bridge or driving across it. For whatever reason, that brief period of time is missing from my memory. I recall telling Ramon to get off at the Pearl Street exit, and the reason we had to was that the roadway of the bridge was being used by thousands of people fleeing from lower Manhattan, but I have no recollection of driving through the throng of people. When we got off we hooked a U-turn at the end of the ramp and pulled onto Avenue of the Finest. This road is next to 1 Police Plaza, which is the headquarters for the NYPD and the building that we worked out of. The streets were filled with responding police personnel. I told Ramon to park the car so we could find out if there was a rescue plan being implemented.

I always regretted stopping at 1PP. It was one of those *in-retrospect* moments which I felt was a dumb decision. I was searching for a coordinated plan, but what I found was a sea of cops and a barely functioning command structure in a state of utter chaos.

No one seemed to know what was going on, but what shocked me most was seeing the senior ranking officers, Inspectors and above, running around like idiots. You could see the panic, because it was manifesting itself in what I could only describe as ranting and raving. One person would tell you to do one thing, the next person would ask why you did that, and the next person would tell you to do something completely different.

I had an Inspector, the military equivalent of a full bird Colonel, tell me, and several other cops I was with, that we would get a complaint, an official reprimand, because we were standing on the *wrong corner*.

At this point I wasn't sure if I would make it through the day, so I told him: "knock your socks off" and walked away. I'll leave the colorful name I inserted at the end of that sentence out of this book.

At one point, I heard that the brass were worried that there would be an attack on 1PP and there was certainly some merit to those fears. At the time the Communications Division was housed there and right next to HQ was the AT&T building with all their equipment. A single attack would have knocked out all emergency communications. Little did we know, this would be rendered a *moot point* shortly, when the North Tower, and its entire communications array, collapsed and knocked out radio and cellular reception.

Shortly thereafter, I located several members of my command, including my Lieutenant, Paul Murphy. Once I found him, I fell under his chain of command and had to follow orders. We began rendering aid to people and assisting them in evacuating from the area. I don't recall when the last wave came, but it seemed as if it had lasted for hours. After the crush of people were gone, the area became like a ghost town, with only police personnel allowed in the area.

After things calmed down, they assigned us to a security checkpoint at the corner of Madison and St. James. Ramon and a couple of others had gone to the equipment section in HQ where they could get raid jackets, emblazoned with NYPD on them, as none of us had anything but our police shields to identify ourselves. As crazy as things were at that moment, quick visual identification seemed prudent. He came back holding an assortment of jackets and hats, which wouldn't have been too bad if the jacket I ended up with wasn't a 3XL. I looked like a little kid who'd stolen his big brother's coat.

Residents of the area were being told to stay in-doors and businesses were closing up since there were no customers. There was a Rite-Aid drugstore at our checkpoint and they were nice enough to come out to tell us they were closing. Not knowing how long we would be there, we bought what we could. I focused on my priorities and picked up several more packs of cigarettes and a Mars bar. We already had a supply of water bottles that someone had dropped off.

And then we waited.

I do remember someone coming by at one point and handing us painter's masks. I looked at it and just stuffed it in my jacket pocket. I was under no illusions and I knew that paper masks were useless in these conditions. Besides, the damage had already done. By this time we had ingested copious amounts of thick smoke that was laden with particles ranging from gypsum, to asbestos, to human remains.

And still we waited.

By the late afternoon only 7 World Trade Center remained and it finally collapsed at around 5:30 p.m.

Early on we were assigned to a Captain who was supervising our sector. She would come by occasionally and I, along with a few others, would question her about getting sent over to the site to help dig. Having a dozen cops assigned to a checkpoint on a deserted intersection seemed like overkill. Freeing up even half of us to go search for survivors seemed like a much more worthwhile task. At one point she came back and told us, in a clearly dejected voice, that she had been unequivocally instructed to *stop asking*.

Later that evening she came by as we were all talking. Everyone was trying to figure out what the hell was going on and scrambling to get any information from what was now being referred to as *Ground Zero*. She mentioned that she wanted to go, but they would not release anyone. I pulled her to the side and said something to the effect of: "*If you want to go, I'll go with you. If anyone asks what happened, I'll just say that I left my post and you came looking for me.*"

"*You'd do that?*" she asked.

"*Yes,*" I replied.

I was more than willing to take a complaint if it meant I could finally do *something* to help, rather than standing around feeling useless.

She told my Lieutenant that we would be back. From 1 Police Plaza to Ground Zero was only about a half dozen blocks. We headed south on Madison and then walked west on Frankfort until we got to Park Row. I'm not sure what I was expecting when we got to Park Row, but I wasn't prepared for it.

I tell people to imagine what it would be like walking in a blizzard, but then realize that it was seventy degrees outside.

The city was quiet, no cars, no people. A layer of thick gray ash covered everything and the streets were eerily lit by the hue of the overhead street lamps. I remember as we made our way past a Starbucks that there was a lone woman's heeled shoe standing upright in the ash. It was as if whoever had been wearing it had slipped out of it during her escape from the city and was too terrified to retrieve it. I remember there was an RMP, what we call a marked patrol car, with the windows smashed out.

Everything looked so surreal, like a scene out of some post-apocalyptic horror movie.

We crossed over Broadway and made our way down Vesey Street, past St. Paul's Chapel. I was happy to see it was actually still standing. St. Paul's was built in 1764, and it is where President George Washington attended services between 1789 and 1790, when New York City served as the nation's first capital. His pew is still there, along with a painting of the great seal of the United States directly above it.

32

As we continued down Vesey street, nothing could have ever prepared me for the sight which was about to greet me.

During my years in the Intelligence Division, I had spent countless hours at the World Trade Center complex. The United States Secret Service's New York Field Office had originally been located at 6 World Trade Center until it moved to 7 World Trade Center. In addition, I had been up to the observation deck on many occasions with visiting dignitaries and law enforcement officials. I knew the entire complex like the back of my hand.

As we passed St. Paul's, and made our way toward Church Street, the image that greeted us was no longer familiar to me, but something which resembled a scene from Dante's Inferno.

A thick blanket of acrid smoke hung in the air, while the night sky was lit by an eerie combination of portable lights and fires. Rescue personnel made their way through the debris covered streets, which were littered with the charred remains of police cars, fire trucks, and ambulances.

As we made our way past the remains of 5 World Trade Center, I could make out a partial section of the North Tower's façade. The fragile aluminum sheathing rising from the rubble was a ghostly reminder of all that we had lost.

CHAPTER THREE
(The Aftermath)

To fully understand the magnitude of what happened on the morning of September 11th, 2001, you have to go back in time to 1968, when construction first began on the World Trade Center complex.

The iconic *Twin Towers* were at the crossroads of the bustling World Financial Center and Wall Street. They also served as one of the preeminent tourist attractions in the city and became one of its most recognized symbols. In fact, it could be argued that the Towers were the *heart* of New York City.

Ask anyone who had visited New York City about the skyline, prior to the September 11th Attack, and inevitably the majority would recount how they looked up at them in awe, as they majestically stood at the southern tip of Manhattan. If you look at any movie or television show set in the city, you are almost certain to see them depicted in the background.

But the sixteen-acre *super-block* looked much different back in the early Dutch explorer days. Back then, the area that comprised the western portion of the World Trade Center site was originally *under* the Hudson River.

At that time, the river's shoreline was near Greenwich and Dey streets. It was on this shoreline, in November 1613, that Dutch explorer Adriaen Block's ship, the *Tyger*, burned at the waterline and forced him to winter-over on the island. As a result, Block and his crew built the first European settlement in what would become known, a decade later, as New Amsterdam. Three hundred years later, in 1916, the remains of the *Tyger* were discovered during excavation work.

Then, in 2010, the remains of a second ship, from the eighteenth century, were located during excavation work at the former World Trade Center site. They found the ship just south of where the Towers used to stand and about 20 feet below the surface.

This proximity to the Hudson River posed unique engineering issues when construction of the World Trade Center was first undertaken. Because the ground in lower Manhattan was largely landfill, engineers had to dig down nearly seventy feet to reach bedrock and have a solid foundation to erect the towers. Then, in order to *seal* the lower levels, and keep water from the Hudson River out of the foundation, they created a type of reverse *bathtub*.

They achieved this by first excavating a three-foot-wide trench down to the bedrock. As dirt and rock were removed, they were replaced by a slurry mixture of water and bentonite, an absorbent aluminium phyllosilicate clay which expanded when wet, to plug any holes along the side of the trench. After they completed this, they lowered a twenty-two ton, seven-story-high, steel cage into the trench. Once secured in place, they used a long pipe to feed concrete into the trench which then displaced the slurry. It took one hundred and fifty of these *trench segments*, spanning an area of two blocks wide and four blocks long, to secure the site's foundation for construction.

Work first began on 1 World Trade Center (North Tower) in 1968 and then 2 World Trade Center (South Tower) the following year and they were finished in 1970 and 1971, respectively. As originally designed, the towers were supposed to be only 80 stories tall, but, to meet the Port Authority's requirement for 10,000,000 square feet of office space, they had to be increased to 110 stories. Because of this, the designers were hit with a major issue: The taller the building, the more elevators that would be needed to service it, requiring more space-consuming elevator banks. To circumvent this issue, they drew inspiration from the New York City subway system. They created a new system with two *sky lobbies*, located on the 44th and 78th floors, where riders could switch from a large-capacity express elevator to a local elevator. The design allowed them to stack local elevators within the same central elevator shaft and increased usable office space on each floor from sixty to seventy-five percent. There were a total of 239 elevators, including one that was considered the fastest in the United States.

One unique fact about the tower's exterior design was that it came about because of lead architect Minoru Yamasaki's fear of heights and his desire to make future occupants feel *secure*. He created tall, but very narrow, windows which were only eighteen inches wide. As someone who does not have an affinity for heights, and who looked out those windows many times, I can confirm that the small width, coupled with the protruding aluminum-alloy façade, gave a visual impression of depth and strength.

At the time they were the largest buildings in the world, with each building coming in at just over 1,360 feet. Over the course of the next several years five more buildings would be added to the site, but it didn't stop at ground level. Below the glistening towers was a vast, nearly seven story, underground complex that included a shopping mall and a hub station for various mass transit entities, including the New York City transit system and the Port Authority's PATH trains.

Once completed, the World Trade Center complex would boast nearly 13.5 million square feet of office space, which accommodated over fifty thousand workers and welcomed almost a quarter of a million daily visitors.

It was these numbers that came to mind when I heard the first call go out over the radio for body bags. The full weight of what had happened finally hit me: *The death toll would be staggering*.

Initially, media reports estimated that the death toll could be in the tens of thousands and there was no reason to discount those reports.

There are no words that can properly describe Ground Zero. Photos and video cannot convey the sheer massiveness of the pile. The collapsed buildings were unstable and engineers feared that the weight of trucks or cranes would cause the wreckage to shift and collapse again; so rescuers had to use a bucket brigade approach to remove the rubble, as they valiantly searched for victims.

As the minutes became hours, and then days turned to weeks, the hopes of rescuing victims turned into the grim reality that it had become an operation to recover the bodies of those who had been lost. Of all the people that were still in the towers when they collapsed, only twenty were pulled out alive.

The last victim rescued was Genelle Guzman McMillan, a Port Authority secretary, who had been at her desk on the 64th floor of the North Tower when the first plane had hit. She made it as far as the 13th floor when it collapsed. She remained buried for twenty-seven hours with her head pinned between two pieces of concrete and her legs covered in pieces of a stairway. Only her left hand was free.

Hour after hour, she fervently prayed to God to spare her; to give her a chance to live a more meaningful life.

On the morning of September 12th, she said that she heard the faint sound of voices and sirens. She called out for help, but said that her voice was barely a whisper. Suddenly, she felt a hand grab hers.

"*I'm down here,*" she shouted. "*Can you see me? Please help me.*"

The hand squeezed hers and a warm, male voice said: "*I've got you. My name's Paul and you're going to be OK.*"

McMillan was subsequently rescued and spent five weeks in the hospital. Later she had the opportunity to meet with and thank her rescuers. She asked about Paul, but she was told that there was no one there that day by that name.

Who Paul was remains a mystery, but to her he was her '*angel in the rubble.*'

It's my personal belief that *Paul* actually was a guardian angel, sent to provide comfort to her until the rescuers reached her.

Then there was the *Miracle of Stairwell B.*

Sixteen people, a bookkeeper, an office temp, an engineer, a Port Authority cop, and twelve FDNY firemen, survived inside the collapse of the World Trade Center, and they were all in Stairwell B of the North Tower.

Josephine Harris, a Port Authority bookkeeper, had made it down to the 20th floor, from the 73rd floor, but physically couldn't go any farther. That was when she encountered FDNY Captain Jay Jonas, of Ladder Company 6 in Chinatown, and his men. Harris had suffered injuries after being hit by a car a few months earlier, and after making the fifty floor trek she was crying and couldn't walk. One of Jonas' men asked him what they should do with her. Jonas already knew the South Tower had collapsed and that they needed to evacuate quickly, but now he had a decision to make: *save six lives or one?*

He looked at Harris and said, *"Well, all right, let's take her with us."*

They made it as far as the 5th floor, supporting her as they descended the staircase, but Harris could no longer move on her own. They paused and began looking for a chair that they could use to carry her the remaining way down, but couldn't locate one. That's when they encountered PAPD K-9 Officer David Lim.

A Port Authority captain yelled at Lim to get moving, but he replied that the captain should *"go ahead."* With Lim's help, they continued to carry Harris down and made it to the 4th floor, which is when they felt the *wind.*

Long before they heard the noise, they felt the rush of air come down the stairwell, as the floors above them pancaked and the North Tower collapsed. A moment later they were thrown about, with one firefighter ending up being lifted into the air and blown down three flights.

For several hours they searched for an escape from the fourth floor. When the smoke and dust cleared, they could make out sunshine coming through the cracks and realized that there was nothing left above them.

The slower timing of their descent, caused by their encounter with Harris, meant that they were not in the lobby of the North Tower when it collapsed, where many others perished. The captain, whom Lim had told to go ahead while he helped evacuate Harris, perished in the collapse.

They called Harris their 'guardian angel.'

Again, they lived because of the physical limitations Harris was under because of her previous accident. I'm sure at the time that she was hit by that car she didn't realize that it was a *good thing*.

Eventually, the pile stabilized enough that construction crews could begin using excavators and other heavy equipment. Over one hundred thousand truckloads, comprising approximately two million tons of rubble, were hauled to the Staten Island landfill, where every one of them was sifted through for remains. On May 30th, 2002, the recovery effort came to a close.

Despite the initial belief that the death toll would be in the *tens of thousands* of people, the actual number of persons killed at the World Trade Center was listed as 2,753. This included:

- 2,184 - Civilians (WTC)
- 422 - First Responders
- 127 - Passengers (Flt AA11 & UA175)
- 20 - Flight Crew (Flt AA11 & UA175)

I should note that these numbers do not include those who became sick afterward from the toxins at Ground Zero. At present there are roughly 80,000 people, civilians and first responders, who are being treated for medical conditions and that number is only likely to grow.

According to the Centers for Disease Control and Prevention (CDC), about 400,000 people are believed to have been exposed to toxic contaminants, or suffered injury or trauma, because of the attack and building collapses.

So what accounted for this substantial difference?

Well, the first plane struck the North Tower at 8:46 a.m., just as most employees were arriving for work. Because of this, many of them remained outside watching as the nightmare unfolded ninety floors above them. As I mentioned earlier, fifty thousand people worked at the World Trade Center and most of them, around thirty-five thousand, would have been at their desks by 9:00 a.m. The first plane also stuck before the observation deck opened at 9:30 a.m., so all the visitors waiting to go up were in the lobby.

Of the 2,184 civilians lost, 2,016 were in the buildings above the affected floors (1,402 in the North Tower above floor 93 and 614 in the South Tower above floor 75).

I point this out, not to minimize the loss of any life, but to showcase how a mere fourteen minutes prevented the need for those *tens of thousands* of body bags.

One account that hit home with me, being a father, was the Cantor Fitzgerald employee who arrived to work later than normal because he had forgotten to do a book order with his son. The twenty extra minutes spent that morning, filling out the form with his child, kept him from being at his desk on the 101st floor.

Or the Morgan Stanley executive who took a rare cigarette break with a co-worker. According to her, she never took a break before noon, yet this morning was different. She was heading down when the plane struck. Moments after she made the fateful decision to take the elevator down to the lobby, a fireball ripped through her office.

Then there was the United Airlines flight attendant who had wanted to work her usual trip from Boston to Los Angeles that month. In August, when she was scheduling her September flights, she accidentally inverted two numbers and ended up with the wrong schedule. When she realized the mistake, she was able to trade flights with other attendants for every flight except for Flight 175 on 9/11. On September 10th, she logged into the airline's computer system and again tried to request that flight, but the system froze up. When it had finally processed her request, it was one minute past the airline's deadline for such changes and was rejected. That morning she was on a shuttle bus with another flight attendant who told her he had gotten called in for the L.A. flight. He later perished.

An employee at Marsh & McLennan, who worked on the 96th floor of the World Trade Center's North Tower, had stopped at the post office on his way to work, before getting on the subway. When he tried to switch to the A train, which was an express, it was too crowded. Being claustrophobic, he got back onto the local train and ended up being late. By the time he arrived, Flight 11 had already struck.

When you look beyond the tragic loss of life, there are many tales of miracles that occurred that day.

Some survivors don't believe that they were saved because of divine intervention, but attribute it to just being *lucky*. That is their choice, but as I like to tell people, *"Just because you don't believe in God, doesn't mean He doesn't believe in you."*

As for me, I am more than willing to accept that my delay that fateful morning was by *divine intervention*. It was something that I had not truly appreciated until Ramon pointed out that had I not quit smoking the week prior, I would have already had the cigarettes on me and there would have been no need to stop. Add that to the fact that the first store was out of my brand and it isn't hard to argue that *someone* was looking out for us that morning. Had I not quit, or the first store had my brand, we would have been pulling up to the South Tower when it collapsed.

CHAPTER FOUR

(The Blame Game)

I don't remember exactly when I first heard the question, as to where God was on 9/11, but I recall that it was a relatively short time after the attack. Considering the magnitude of the horror we had just gone through, it seemed like a reasonable question and I struggled to find an answer.

Over the years it has become almost second nature to question why God either allowed something to happen or why God did not do something to fix it. It rears its ugly head almost immediately after some horrific attack, as people desperately try to make heads or tails of what has occurred. While some people ask the question in earnest, as they struggle with finding some semblance of understanding amid the chaos, others say it mockingly. It is as if they derive some perverse thrill, through the pain of others, while they impugn God.

It is not an attitude that is limited strictly to atheists, but this disconnect from God is alive and well within media, entertainment and political circles as well.

Those of you alive in the 60s might recall the very provocative Time magazine cover asking the question: *Is God Dead*? But it wasn't all that long ago that a major newspaper publication ran the cover: *God Isn't Fixing This*, in response to politicians offering their prayers to the victims of the San Bernardino terror attacked.

It is not even just limited to horrific attacks. No, the questions about God abound in everyday issues such as *homelessness, abuse, starvation, disease* and *murder*. It seems that every time we are faced with a tragedy, some people take the opportunity to either dismiss the idea of God outright or to mock Him for not caring enough.

But is that really fair?

Is God some unfeeling, uncaring, detached deity? Is He too caught-up in Himself to care about His petty little creation?

The more I thought about the original question, the more I was met with an even bigger one: *Why does God always get blamed*?

No matter what happens in the world, the recrimination, as to why He didn't do anything to stop it, always arrives back on God's doorstep.

In a way I can understand the frustration. After twenty-plus years in law enforcement I have seen far too much suffering, tragedy and death. I have literally had a front-row seat to all manner of man's inhumanity to man. They will tell you that you have to leave those things in your locker at the end of a shift, but you can't. You just learn how to cope as best as you can. Sadly, not every cop can do this and they become yet another victim.

I know that it is very popular these days to blame police officers for a whole host of societal ills, but a law enforcement officer's job is incredibly difficult. There are simply no routine days. That's not to say that every day is spent running from one job to another. Some areas might be like that, but most aren't. One of the best analogies I ever heard about police work was that it was ninety percent boredom and ten percent sheer terror. The only problem was that you never knew when you were going to encounter that sheer terror, such as what we witnessed on September 11th.

I was having a discussion with someone and they smugly informed me that the empirical data did not support the claim that police officers had a particularly tough job. They cited the fact that many jobs, including loggers and fisherman, actually had higher ratios of *on the job* fatalities. I listened politely until they were finished lecturing me on my factual ignorance and then I replied.

I informed them they were *statistically correct*, but that didn't mean they had made their point. I agreed that many jobs, including those of the aforementioned loggers and fisherman, were inherently dangerous, but the numbers did not explain everything. To the best of my knowledge, neither profession was ever accosted by gun-toting oak trees or knife-wielding salmon. Nor did either profession have to comfort said tree or salmon after their off-spring were innocently gunned down in a gang drive-by.

While it is true that other jobs might be more dangerous, those are most often *known* dangers. A lineman, working up on a pole, understands the danger from the amount of electricity coursing through the line and can take precautions to ensure his safety. He doesn't fear for his life when he drives underneath every power line. A cop on the other hand understands that they are always a target. Simply walking into a store to purchase a soda, on a hot summer day, could end up in a shootout with a would-be robber. A cop can never take anything for granted.

So in a *very small way* I can understand the frustration that God might feel at times.

Before we can answer the question, as to *where God was* on 9/11, we first have to ask ourselves what *we know about Him*.

I want you to take everything you think you know about God, put it in a box, seal it up and throw it away. The idea that we earnestly believe that we can understand God is rife with problems.

The Bible states clearly, in **Isaiah 55: 8-9**, "*For my thoughts are not your thoughts, neither are your ways my ways,*" declares the LORD. "*As the heavens are higher than the earth, so are my ways higher than your ways and my thoughts than your thoughts.*" (NIV)

So where does this disconnect stem from? Well, if truth be told, it rests within all of us.

Who among you reading this book has been the *bad parent*? Raise your hand.

I certainly know that I have.

Now, does that mean I am really a bad parent? The answer, as I am sure it is in your case, is a resounding: *No.*

That doesn't mean I am a perfect parent, but I have never intended to cause harm to my children. In truth, most of the allegations surrounding my *bad parenting* come from actively trying to protect my kids from their bad choices.

As parents, one of the hardest things that we must grudgingly accept is that we ultimately cannot save our children from themselves. As hard as it may be at times, we must accept the fact that all of us are born with free will, even our children. That is not always easy to accept, especially when you are watching someone you brought into this world making very poor life decisions.

Can you stop them?

I guess you could try and lock them in a windowless room until they come to their senses, but keeping someone a prisoner is not a particularly strong foundation to build a loving relationship on. It is also generally frowned upon by the courts, who'll most likely provide you with a similar accommodation should your young charge ever escape.

So what do you do?

Well, you do your best, but you also have to be willing to open the door and let them fly, even when it tears your heart apart. The best example we have of this is in **Luke 15: 11-32**. It is commonly referred to as the *Parable of the Prodigal Son*.

In this parable, Jesus tells the story of a wealthy man who had two sons. The younger asks for his inheritance and leaves his father's house, but it is not too long before he has wasted his money and is destitute. After much consideration, he returns to his home in hopes that he can appeal to his father and at least be made one of his hired servants. In his heart the young man believes that his family relationship is over, but even while he was still afar, his father rushed out and embraced him. Much to the young man's surprise, his father welcomed him back into his home and celebrated his return with an extravagant party. However, the older son was indignant and refused to participate. The father then explains to the older son, "*Your brother was dead, and is alive again. He was lost and is found.*"

The request by the younger son, for his share of his father's inheritance, was the equivalent of wishing that his father was dead. Yet, after receiving it, his life does not lead to the success he envisioned. Eventually, he ends up being an indentured servant and finds himself envying his father's servants.

The significance of this parable needs to truly be understood. It is one of three parables (the other two being the *Lost Sheep* and the *Lost Coin*) dealing with loss and redemption.

As a parent, I am sure that many of us can imagine being in the very same position as that father and have probably uttered the infamous line: "*Told you so.*"

Yet, this story is as much about the father, as it is the prodigal son. In this parable, the father does not utter those words. Instead, he throws an elaborate celebration in honor of the return of his child. It speaks to the boundless *mercy* of God and His refusal to limit the measure of His *grace*.

Let that sink in for a moment.

Does that sound like the qualities of an *uncaring* or *distant* God?

I am reminded of the passage in **2 Peter 3:9**, "*The Lord is not slow in keeping his promise, as some understand slowness. Instead he is patient with you, not wanting anyone to perish, but everyone to come to repentance.*" (NIV)

Time and again we are given numerous examples of God's unlimited love for us. So if God truly only wants the best for us, why do these bad things continue to plague our world?

Well, the short answer is: Us.

As I mentioned before, my career in law enforcement has provided me with countless examples of just how cruel we can be to each other. I've lost count of the many ways that we hurt and kill one another. Sometimes it is for personal reasons, sometimes it is professional, and occasionally it is just for kicks.

If we take a step back we can see it transcend the local setting and manifest itself upon the global stage.

War, starvation, genocide, and terror are just some of the ways we hurt our fellow human beings.

Maybe it is time to stop blaming God for every bad thing that happens in our world and start putting the blame where it truly belongs: at *humanities* doorstep.

CHAPTER FIVE

(Sin)

I would venture to say that almost everyone who sits down to read the Bible has the best of intentions, so they naturally jump right in at page one.

Genesis 1, "*In the beginning, God created the heavens and the earth.*" (NIV)

It is a very powerful opening statement.

In one succinct sentence it introduces us to the awesome power and majesty that is God.

God created..... *Everything.*

The other night, I stood out on my deck and stared up at Jupiter. It was a small, but very bright, star in the south-western sky. I paused for a moment and looked around, taking in the multitude of other celestial bodies that hung in the evening sky. Living out in the country, without the ambient light found in cities, allows for a much better view.

I must admit that it was impressive, but it still wasn't very accurate. The countless stars that blanket the night sky are only a tiny fraction of what we can see with the naked eye.

The Hubble Space Telescope has revealed about 100 *billion* galaxies in the universe, but scientists admit that this number is likely to increase to 200 billion, as space telescope technology improves.

The reality is, we do not understand just how big the universe is, but God does, because He created it all.

Do you want to feel tiny?

It would take 1.3 million Earths to fit within the Sun.

That's impressive, isn't it?

Actually, it isn't. Not when you consider that you could fit 9.3 *billion* of our Suns into the red supergiant star known as *VY Canis Majoris*.

Most of us pay little attention when we glance up at the evening sky. If by chance you do, there is no way that you can't help but feel just how *small* we truly are. Yet, despite the fragility of our lives, we have this exceptional God who desires to have a relationship with us, but we often act like the petulant child who knows better.

Consider for a moment that the shortest question in the Bible is also God's first question: "*Ayeka*?"

In **Genesis 3:9**, Adam and Eve had just eaten the fruit of the forbidden tree and, sensing God's presence in the Garden of Eden, they hid among the trees. While they were in hiding, God asked Adam that one-word Hebrew question, *Ayeka*? Which in English translates to: "*Where are you*?"

Unfortunately, this simple, and yet very poignant, question is almost universally glossed over by most readers. So let me put it to you this way: Do you think God, the author of all of creation, the great *I Am*, honestly didn't know where Adam was?

Of course He did.

God knew exactly where Adam was. He was asking Adam if *he* knew where he was.

The biblical foundation for our free will lies in the fall into sin by Adam and Eve, which occurred after their *willfully chosen* disobedience to God. Since the Garden of Eden, each of us has come into this world with sin in our hearts and, left to our own choices, we are inclined to turn away from God.

Why is this?

Admittedly, I honestly don't know. It is something that remains a mystery to me, not that I haven't pondered this. I spent years believing that I was an altruistic person and then one day I had an epiphany: *I'm a sinner.*

That's sometimes a tough thing to admit, but it's still the truth. In the five plus decades of my life I have lied, stole, cheated, and I've hurt those closest to me. I have done the very things that I would not tolerate from others. Yet when I do them, I can somehow rationalize it.

You see, the problem with having free will is that we get to choose how we act and most times it is not good. I am ashamed to admit that I have often been the farthest thing from a *Christian*.

Now, some claim that God's omniscience and the theory of free will are incompatible, but I disagree with this. In the last chapter I asked you to take everything you thought you knew about God and discard it. The reason for this is that I think we, as humans, erroneously try to *humanize* God, so we can make sense of Him. I believe this is rooted deeply in man's hubris.

I've lost count of the number of times I have heard people say that if God were really *omniscient, omnipotent,* and *omnipresent*, then He knew I would do this and therefore I didn't have a choice in the matter. Some use this as a defense for what they have done wrong, contending that they were made this way and therefore they are just doing what they were *predestined* to do.

Rabbi Moses ben Maimon (Maimonides), was a 12th century Sephardic Jewish philosopher who became one of the most prolific and influential Torah scholars of the Middle Ages. He postulated the question: *"Does God know or does He not know that a certain individual will be good or bad? If thou sayest 'He knows', then it necessarily follows that the man is compelled to act as God knew beforehand how he would act, otherwise God's knowledge would be imperfect."*

Now, I am not claiming to be on the same theological level as Rabbi Maimonides, but that doesn't mean that I can't take fault with his assessment. My primary criticism is that it once again tries to imply that God is somehow constrained by accepted human norms.

Many years ago my wife shared with me a saying she'd been told: *"We see the snapshot of our life, but God sees the movie."*

In essence, our ability to see things is limited to the immediate present and our past, yet God has seen things from the beginning to the end. We are reminded of this in both the Old and New Testaments, first in **Isaiah 44:6**, *"Thus saith the LORD the King of Israel, and his redeemer the LORD of hosts; I am the first, and I am the last; and beside me there is no God."* (KJV) And then in **Revelation 21:6**, *"He said to me: 'It is done. I am the Alpha and the Omega, the Beginning and the End.'"* (NIV)

Are we to believe that God, the Alpha and the Omega, the First and the Last, the Creator of the Heavens and Earth, sits on His majestic throne and thinks: *"Damn, I didn't see that one coming...."*

No, I believe this is firmly rooted in man's need for control. We see this played out all the time when one theologian or another comes forward to claim they have figured out when the *end of days* will be. Predictions of apocalyptic events, which would usher in the second coming of Christ, have been made almost since the Book of Revelation was written by John in the first century. Now it is easy to chalk up most of these predictions as ramblings, but among those predicting the apocalypse are several well-known, well-respected, theologians and scientists including: Pope Innocent III, Martin Luther, Christopher Columbus, Sir Isaac Newton, Rasputin, Nostradamus, Pat Robertson, Menachem Schneerson, Jerry Falwell, and Harold Camping.

Humanity has an inherent desire to feel as if we know it all, even when it comes to God, but should we?

In **Matthew 24:36**, Jesus says unequivocally: *"But of that day and that hour knoweth no man, no, not the angels which are in heaven, neither the Son, but the Father."* (KJV)

It seems quite arrogant to think we could figure out this grand mystery, when Jesus admits that even He does not know the appointed time.

As we saw in **Isaiah 55: 8**, God tells us that *His ways are not our ways*. So how could we ever presume to know how God sees things?

One theory, which I am inclined to believe, is that we do not understand God's perception of time.

I previously mentioned **2 Peter 3:9**, in which the writer explained, "*The Lord is not slow in keeping his promise, as some understand slowness.*" But in the passage just before that, **2 Peter 3:8,** it is written: "*But do not forget this one thing, dear friends: With the Lord a day is like a thousand years, and a thousand years are like a day.*" (NIV)

In his book, *Mere Christianity*, C. S. Lewis argues that God is actually *outside* time and therefore does not *foresee* events, but rather He observes them all at once.

Lewis postulates: "*But suppose God is outside and above the time-line. In that case, what we call tomorrow is visible to Him in just the same way as what we call today. All the days are Now for Him. He does not remember you doing things yesterday, He simply sees you doing them: because, though you have lost yesterday, He has not. He does not foresee you doing things tomorrow, He simply sees you doing them: because, though tomorrow is not yet there for you, it is for Him. You never supposed that your actions at this moment were any less free because God knows what you are doing. Well, He knows your tomorrow's actions in just the same way—because He is already in tomorrow and can simply watch you. In a sense, He does not know your action till you have done it: but then the moment at which you have done it is already Now for Him.*"

To expound on this briefly, and rather primitively, it would be like a parent putting a plate of salad and a plate of cookies in front of us and asking us to choose what we want. Of course we have a *choice*, but that doesn't mean that our parent doesn't already *know* what we are going to choose. And if the cookies we choose (with our free will) represent sin, can He also not use that to teach us something?

To take it just a step further, imagine a few months down the road and you're faced with a dentist appointment because of a cavity. Would it be inconceivable to not imagine that the conversation going a bit like this, 'Well, I allowed you to choose the cookies, because I knew you'd get a cavity and have to endure the dentist's drill, but I also knew that it would have a profound impact on you and cause you to avoid eating bad things and save you from even more dental work.'

It might be difficult for us to wrap our head around this concept, but that is because we are not God. We are just humans, but are we alone in our sinful nature?

CHAPTER SIX

(Satan)

Angra Mainyu, Belial, Beelzebub, Sataneal, Diabolo, Shaitan, Baphomet, Mephistopheles, Lucifer, Moloch, Yaotzin, Emma-O, the Deceiver, the Accuser, the Tempter, the Dragon, the Serpent, the Prince of the Power of Air.

He is referred to by many different names, but they all refer to one entity: Satan.

So what do you think of when you hear the name of Satan?

When I was younger, I envisioned a dark, evil looking figure with horns, cloven-hoofed feet, a pointed tail, and who smelled of brimstone. I'm sure most of us grew up with some manner of *cartoonish* character in our heads. Even around Halloween it is still common to see some farcical interpretation of this very serious entity.

As I grew older, I wondered why this image had been reduced to such a seemingly insignificant caricature. It begged the question: "What exactly do we know about Satan?"

It turns out that we know an impressive amount about him, at least if we take the time to do the research. The Bible refers to him more than any other evil entity. In fact, Jesus mentions him twenty-five times. If Christ felt it important enough to mention him, then I think it is best if we take the time to acquaint ourselves with this spiritual enemy.

In **Matthew 12:24**, he is referred to as the '*prince of demons.*' This is an important distinction to note. While he surely holds a place of prominence in the spiritual realm, and is the undisputed ruler of a host of evil spirits, we must never forget that he is still *subservient* to God.

John 12:31, refers to him as the *'ruler of this world'* and he exercises massive authority over the system of things opposed to God.

Ephesians 2:2, calls him the *'prince of the power of the air.'* In this case, the *air* refers to this earthly realm.

1 John 5:19, adds: "the whole world is under the control of the evil one."

2 Cor. 4:4, describes him as the *'god of this world,'* who has blinded the minds of the unbelievers, in order to keep them from seeing the light of the Gospels.

All-in-all, the Bible refers to him fifty-two (52) times as *Satan* (adversary or opposer) and thirty-five (35) times as the *Devil* (accuser or slanderer). Other descriptions include:

The evil one (John 17:15)

A roaring lion (1 Peter 5:8)

Abaddon (destroyer, Rev. 9:11)

A great red dragon (Rev. 12:3)

That ancient serpent (Rev. 12:9)

Looking at these references, one cannot help but surmise that we are not dealing with some mythical creature at all. No, our antagonist is quite real and he is not the marginalized cartoon villain that so many make him out to be. He is a powerful, destructive, amazingly clever, and an intrinsically evil entity who has a host of lesser, demonic spirits under his control.

Yet, despite the obvious examples of the danger posed by Satan, I am sometimes amazed at how quickly people are to blame God for all the dreadful things that happen in life. Rarely have I ever heard anyone come out and rebuke Satan. Seriously, think about it for a moment. When was the last time you heard someone say: "Why did Satan cause that tragedy?"

It reminds me of the famous line from the movie, The Usual Suspects, when Kevin Spacey's character says "*The greatest trick the devil ever pulled was to convince the world he didn't exist.*"

But that wasn't always the case.

I remember when the movie *The Exorcist* was released in 1973. Full disclosure: I haven't and will not see it. It might sound strange, considering all the real-world evil I have seen, but something about it just screams: 'Oh, hell no,' deep inside me. But I know enough about it to understand that it depicts the spiritual, psychological, and moral warfare that goes on daily.

There is a sinister darkness about the movie that is at odds with the *normal* horror films that Hollywood produces. Most of them are over-the-top spectacles that rarely can hold my attention. Maybe it is because *The Exorcist* has its foundation in reality. In explaining why he wrote the book, the author, William Peter Blatty, said that he "*hoped it would make people think positively about the existence of God.*" Blatty felt that if there are demons, then there are also angels and life after death.

There is a sound argument that can be made for that belief. My time as an altar boy taught me that the Catholic Church certainly took the matter seriously enough. I recall the first time I saw the exorcism kit in the sacristy. It chilled me to the bone and made me feel *very* uncomfortable. Once I knew what it was, I wouldn't even *look* at it. I just gathered up all the other instruments for the mass and closed the door as quickly as possible.

I have a dear friend, Larry Wilson, who is a paranormal investigator and author. He has spent years going around the country to investigate allegations of hauntings. In my career I have chased down a number of armed individuals and have gone face-to-face with people that I would consider evil, but Larry has faced something entirely different. During his investigations he has identified several hoaxes and simple misidentifications. But while he can explain a large majority of events away, there remain a fair number that cannot be, and it is within those events that we get a glimpse of the supernatural. Larry has shared with me some compelling audio and video evidence and I admit that I am at a loss to explain it.

Even if you discount the vast majority of incidents, there are still many that have no earthly explanation. Once we have ruled out the natural, we must explore the supernatural.

We are mere mortals, and our time on Earth is finite, but accepting that God and Satan exist opens the realm of eternal life. Yet many people are deathly afraid of this possibility, but is this level of fear justified?

In the Gospels of **Mark 1:12-13** and **Luke 4:1-13** they give us insight at how Jesus responded when Satan appeared and tempted Him in the wilderness.

Then Jesus was led by the Spirit into the wilderness to be tempted by the devil. After fasting forty days and forty nights, He was hungry. The tempter came to Him and said, "If You are the Son of God, tell these stones to become bread." But Jesus answered, "It is written: 'Man shall not live on bread alone, but on every word that comes from the mouth of God.'"

Then the devil took Him to the holy city and set Him on the pinnacle of the temple. "If You are the Son of God," he said, "throw Yourself down. For it is written: 'He will command His angels concerning You, and they will lift You up in their hands, so that You will not strike Your foot against a stone.'" Jesus replied, "It is also written: 'Do not put the Lord your God to the test.'"

Again, the devil took Him to a very high mountain and showed Him all the kingdoms of the world and their glory. "All this I will give You," he said, "if You will fall down and worship me." "Away from me, Satan!" Jesus declared. "For it is written: 'Worship the Lord your God and serve Him only.'" Then the devil left Him, and angels came and ministered to Him.

Notice how Satan is portrayed. He is the *tempter*, the *deceiver*, the *accuser*, but we, like Jesus, are ultimately responsible for how *we* respond. Just like Adam and Eve, we have free will to choose, but unlike Jesus we often make the wrong choices.

We are however not alone in our shortcomings and I take some measure of comfort in knowing that even the Apostle Paul, arguably one of the most prolific evangelists of all time, struggled with his own shortcomings and sinful nature.

In discussing the law and sin in **Romans 7: 14-20**, Paul lays out a perfect example of the struggle many of us deal with daily. *"We know that the law is spiritual; but I am unspiritual, sold as a slave to sin. I do not understand what I do. For what I want to do I do not do, but what I hate I do. And if I do what I do not want to do, I agree that the law is good. As it is, it is no longer I myself who do it, but it is sin living in me. For I know that good itself does not dwell in me, that is, in my sinful nature. For I have the desire to do what is good, but I cannot carry it out. For I do not do the good I want to do, but the evil I do not want to do—this I keep on doing. Now if I do what I do not want to do, it is no longer I who do it, but it is sin living in me that does it."* (NIV)

In fact, Paul has much to say about the issues of sin and Satan. Consider the following passages:

1 Corinthians 10:13, *"No temptation has overtaken you except what is common to mankind. And God is faithful; He will not let you be tempted beyond what you can bear. But when you are tempted, He will also provide a way out so that you can endure it."* (NIV)

2 Corinthians 12:7-9, *"Therefore, in order to keep me from becoming conceited, I was given a thorn in my flesh, a messenger of Satan, to torment me. Three times I pleaded with the Lord to take it away from me. But he said to me, 'My grace is sufficient for you, for my power is made perfect in weakness.'"* (NIV)

Satan has been in this world since its creation. He is the bane of our existence, our protagonist, our accuser. In the previous chapter I mentioned how God's first question was to ask where

Adam was, but we attribute the very first question in the Bible to the wily *serpent*.

In **Genesis 3:1**, our fall from grace begins with asking a simple question to Eve: "*Did God really say, 'You must not eat from any tree in the garden?'*"

And therein lies the insidiousness of the devil's attacks. They are not always *demonic* in nature. Not to underestimate Satan's significance in our spiritual battle, but to me Satan is more like that one terrible friend we all have who is always encouraging our poor life-style choices.

Sometimes they come in the form of a question or a feeling. And soon we are internally justifying the things which we know are inherently wrong, yet we choose to do them anyway. The forbidden fruit we *want*, instead of the rule we should *follow*.

Think I am wrong?

Consider for a moment the way humans always tend to *frame* an issue.

When Moses came down from Mount Sinai with the *Ten Commandments*, the laws God gave him, things were pretty straightforward:

- Thou shalt not have strange gods before Me.

- Thou shalt not make to thyself a graven thing, nor the likeness of anything that is in heaven above, or the earth beneath, nor of those things that are in the waters under the earth.

- Thou shalt not take the name of the Lord thy God in vain: for the Lord shall not hold him guiltless that shall take the name of the Lord God in vain.

- Remember that thou keep holy the Sabbath day.

- Honor thy father and thy mother, that thou may be long-lived upon the land which the Lord thy God will give thee.

- Thou shall not kill.

- Thou shall not commit adultery.

- Thou shall not steal.

- Thou shall not bear false witness against thy neighbor.

- Thou shall not covet thy neighbor's house: neither shalt thou desire his wife, nor his servant, nor his handmaid, nor his ox, nor his ass, nor anything that is his.

Ten simple rules, the vast majority of which, I think most people would admit, are pretty much *boiler plate* stuff for living an exemplary life.

Now let's look at an easy one: *Thou shall not kill.*

You would think we would be okay with this straight off, but think again. Human beings seem to have an inherent need to prove that we are *technically* better than the next person, even when it comes to crimes.

Consider for a moment the different classifications of homicide contained in the New York State Penal Law (by felony class).

1. Criminal Negligent Homicide (E)
2. Abortion 2nd degree (E)
3. Abortion 1st degree (D)
4. Vehicular Manslaughter 2nd degree (D)
5. Aggravated Crim. Negligent Homicide (C)
6. Vehicular Manslaughter 1st degree (C)
7. Manslaughter 2nd degree (C)
8. Aggravated Manslaughter 2nd degree (C)
9. Aggravated Vehicular Homicide (B)
10. Manslaughter 1st degree (B)
11. Aggravated Manslaughter 1st degree (B)
12. Murder 2nd degree (A-1)
13. Aggravated Murder (A-1)
14. Murder 1st degree (A-1)

It seemed simple enough when God commanded: *Thou shall not kill*, but we need to feel as if our crime isn't as bad as all those *really bad* people.

If you listen closely, you can almost hear Satan saying: '*Surely God didn't say that........*'

If you take a look at the world we live in today, it seems as if we are intentionally going out of our way to diminish God. In a way it makes sense. By embracing the corporeal, we get to engage in all of the fun with none of the condemnation. By removing Satan from the equation, we can then remove God, and this allows us to be able to live for the moment without repercussions.

You don't have to look very far to see this in application. All throughout our society, forces are in-play to repudiate God and systematically remove Him from our daily lives. We have taken Him out of our schools, places of employment, the public-square, and government. We routinely mock God as being just a fairy tale. Then we go even further and assail those who believe in Him as being weak-minded *simpletons*.

The enlightened folks within the academic, political, and journalism communities, who have *risen above* the religious dogma, are the same ones who have led the charge to legalize drugs, take away parental rights, teach kids that there are no consequences for their abhorrent behavior (crime, abortion, etc), and install government above all other things. Then, when terrible things happen, they use the moment to further vilify God as being uncaring or detached, while they seek to divert attention from themselves.

For folks who don't seem to believe in Him, they sure spend a lot of time denouncing Him.

If we take the time to search-out where the motivation for this behavior lies, we will find it in **Ephesians 2:1-2**, "*As for you, you were dead in your transgressions and sins, in which you used to live when you followed the ways of this world and of the ruler of the kingdom of the air, the spirit who is now at work in those who are disobedient.*" (NIV)

The sad fact is that a growing segment of the population is either overtly following Satan or allowing him to work in their lives. He is always moving about the world, sowing the seeds of anger, hatred, immorality, and violence. Therefore, it is not unusual that we should see these attempts to diminish God. In the end, the absence of God from our daily lives elevates Satan's role in the world.

But in order for us to condemn Satan, for all the pain and hurt that plagues this world, first we have to make the case for God. The Bible is either authentic or it is not. In the end, we cannot have Satan if we do not have God.

The question then becomes: *how do you prove God's existence?*

CHAPTER SEVEN

(The Case for Christ)

The late scientist, Carl Sagan, once said that, *"the absence of evidence is not evidence of absence."*

To put it in laymen's terms: if you look for X, but don't find it, does that prove that there was no X to begin with?

The answer is: ***no***.

The search for evidence is something I am intimately familiar with, thanks to my career in law enforcement. It is a process which can sometimes be easy and other times it is painstakingly frustrating.

When I found myself at my religious crossroads, I had to take pause and consider both what I did and didn't know. Growing up in the Catholic Church they taught me religion, but I didn't *experience* it.

In a way, it was like learning 18th century history. You master the details you need to pass the test, but you never really appreciate the reasons. So when I found myself wondering about the existence of God, it felt normal that I should apply the same investigatory skills that had earned me the coveted NYPD detective shield.

Unfortunately, it seemed an insurmountable task. I mean how does one prove the existence of the *Great I Am*? It's not like you can launch a signal into the sky or pick up a covert *God phone* and have a chat. But as I took a step back I realized that if we couldn't establish direct evidence of the existence of God the Father, perhaps we could establish it through the alleged Son of God: Jesus Christ.

To Christians, Jesus is the *Savior* and the central figure of Christianity. For some Jews He is seen as a *rabbi*, but by the larger religious authority He is viewed as an *apostate*. To Muslims

He is recognized as a messenger of God and the *Messiah* sent to guide the Israelites with a new scripture. Some Hindus consider Jesus to be an *avatar* or a *sadhu*, while some Buddhists regard Jesus as a *bodhisattva*; someone who dedicated His life to the welfare of people. Of the worlds estimated seven billion plus inhabitants, not only do the vast majority believe in some form of monotheism, that is the belief in the existence of one God that created the world, but they also acknowledge the historical existence of Jesus.

I would be remiss if I didn't mention that Jesus is the most mentioned person in the Quran. He is mentioned twenty-five times by the name *Isa*, forty-eight times in the third-person, and thirty-five times in the first-person. Another interesting note is that the Virgin Mary, Jesus' mother, is the only woman mentioned in the Quran by the name Mariam.

So I set everything I knew, or thought I knew, off to the side. I started with the proverbial *blank* notepad and went to work.

Enter: *NEOTWY*

NEOTWY is an acronym they teach you in the early days of the Police Academy. It is formed by using the last letter of *when* (N), *where* (E) *who* (O), *what* (T), *how* (W) and *why* (Y).

The way I looked at it, the death of Jesus was the most infamous murder of all time, so a homicide investigation was the natural place to begin. I set forth to identify the particulars.

Who: Jesus of Nazareth

What: Homicide

When: Approximately AD 33

Where: Jerusalem

Why: Politics / Religion

How: Crucifixion

Obviously, as an investigator, the first thing that you want to know is: *Who is my victim?*

Because we are looking at an investigation that certainly qualifies as an *Extremely Cold Case*, we need to establish if a victim actually existed.

Fortunately for us, virtually all *scholars of antiquity* agree that the *person* of Jesus existed. Although there are differing opinions as to the beliefs and teachings of Jesus, and the accuracy of the biblical accounts, we know that there are two events that have almost universal acceptance: That Jesus was baptized in the Jordan River by John the Baptist and that he was crucified by order of Pontius Pilate, the fifth Roman prefect of the province of Judaea, who served under Emperor Tiberius from AD 26 to 36. These *confirmed* events serve as the evidence we need to establish two fundamental points: That Jesus was an actual person and that He was killed.

So what else do we know about Jesus?

Well, according to scripture, we know that Jesus was born of virgin birth to Mary around 4 BC. Jesus' childhood home is identified in the gospels as the town of Nazareth in Galilee. Although His step-father Joseph appears in descriptions of Jesus' birth, no mention is made of him thereafter. They identify other family members as His brothers James, Joses (also referred to as Joseph), Judas, and Simon. There are sisters who are mentioned, but are not further identified.

We should note that early on in His ministry, His family was not supportive of Him. The Gospel of Mark recounts an incident in Galilee where Jesus' mother and brothers come to get Him because He had come into conflict with His neighbors and religious leaders because of His teachings. He was simultaneously accused of being both crazy and demonically possessed (**Mark 3:22**).

This establishes another fact for us: at this point in His ministry, among those who would know Him the best, He was certainly *not* accepted as the Son of God. So what happened?

Well, by all accounts, Jesus' ministry was short lived. In contrast to His impact on the world, it is generally believed that His teaching only lasted for roughly three years, although the date ranges vary based on Gospel interpretation. It is accepted that his ministry began with His baptism in the Jordon and ended in Jerusalem, following the Last Supper.

In the beginning, Jesus preached around Galilee and it is there that He met His first disciples, who traveled with Him and would eventually form the nucleus of the early Church. Over the course of the next few years, besides His preaching, Jesus performed a number of miracles that were documented in both the Gospels and later in Islamic texts. These supernatural deeds included healings, exorcisms, the resurrection of the dead, and control over nature.

Taken at face value, these miracles would seem to support the contention that Jesus was not just a mere mortal, but we lack the ability to know more about the details. What we know is that they were observed first-hand by Jesus' disciples and other witnesses.

One of the attributed miracles that stood out to me was the account of Jesus walking on water. This event struck a chord with the Gospel writers because they recorded it in three of the four Gospels (Mark, Matthew & John).

The details of the event show that it occurred following the feeding of the five thousand on the shore of the Sea of Galilee. Jesus sent the disciples by ship back to the eastern side of the sea, while He remained behind to pray. When night fell, the ship was coat up in a wind storm. After rowing against it for most of the night, the disciples saw Jesus walking toward them on the sea and they became frightened, but Jesus instructed them not to be afraid. After He entered the ship, the wind ceased, and they arrived at land. The Gospel of Matthew has an additional passage which reads in part:

Matthew 14: 28-31, *"And Peter answered him and said, Lord, if it be thou, bid me come unto thee upon the waters. And He said,*

Come. And Peter went down from the boat, and walked upon the waters to come to Jesus. But when he saw the wind, he was afraid; and beginning to sink, he cried out, saying, Lord, save me. And immediately Jesus stretched forth his hand, and took hold of him, and saith unto him, O thou of little faith, wherefore didst thou doubt?"(KJV)

This is the first of two events surrounding Jesus and the elements. The second occurred one evening, while Jesus and his disciples were crossing the Sea of Galilee in a boat. During the passage, a storm rose up and the waves began breaking over the sides, threatening to sink the boat. Jesus was asleep in the stern and one of the disciples woke him and asked, *"Teacher, don't you care if we drown?"*

The **Gospel of Mark** says: *He got up, rebuked the wind and said to the waves, "Quiet! Be still!" Then the wind died down and it was completely calm. He said to his disciples, "Why are you so afraid? Do you still have no faith?" They were terrified and asked each other, "Who is this? Even the wind and the waves obey him!"* **Mark 4: 39-41** (NIV)

Now it is important to note that on both occasions Jesus admonishes his disciples over their lack of faith.

I think it is impossible for us to either prove or disprove these supernatural events, because in order to prove them one would have to believe in a supernatural world which would not be amenable to historical analysis, yet disproving them would require historical evidence that would be very hard to come by, especially at this late date. Yet, if we accept for the moment the veracity of these accounts, then we can presume that Jesus was endowed with divine properties and was elevated above nature itself. It also shows that, while they followed Him, His core group still had doubts about who Jesus was. This is a particularly relevant fact.

What we know is that the majority of these miraculous events were not only witnessed by a multitude of people, but by the small cadre of followers who would also accompany Him on His fateful trip to Jerusalem.

Now that we have established who our victim was, we must now investigate the circumstances leading up to His demise.

As I stated before, the two things that have almost universal acceptance are that Jesus was baptized and that He was crucified.

From a historical perspective, we know that John the Baptist existed and was an itinerant Jewish preacher. He is revered not just by Christians, but by Muslims alike. The Quran identifies John by the name *Yahya*. So his position that Jesus was the *Lamb of God* is significant.

At the time, many claimed that John was the Messiah, which he openly denied, but in the Gospel of John we learn that his baptismal activities landed him on the radar of the religious leaders in Jerusalem. This resulted in them dispatching Pharisees to question him specifically about these claims.

Finally they [Pharisees'] said, "Who are you? Give us an answer to take back to those who sent us. What do you say about yourself?" John replied in the words of Isaiah the prophet, "I am the voice of one calling in the wilderness, 'Make straight the way for the Lord.'" Now the Pharisees who had been sent questioned him, "Why then do you baptize if you are not the Messiah, nor Elijah, nor the Prophet?" "I baptize with water," John replied, "but among you stands one you do not know. He is the one who comes after me, the straps of whose sandals I am not worthy to untie." **John 1:22-27** (NIV)

This comment from John, about someone greater than him, *who they didn't know*, must have sent shock waves through the religious authority in Jerusalem. The Pharisees and Sadducees were the priests and legal authority of the time and they comprised the ruling class of Jews in Israel. To put it in contemporary terms, they were like the political parties of modern day.

The Sadducees were more elitist and aristocratic than the Pharisees. Sadducees tended to be wealthier and held more prominent positions. The high priest was a Sadducee, as were the chief priests. They also held a majority of the seats in the Sanhedrin, the rabbinical court.

In contrast, the Pharisees were more representative of the common people and had the respect of the masses. While the Sadducees' center of power was the temple in Jerusalem, the Pharisees controlled the smaller synagogues. They were also divided along political lines. Sadducees were seen as being friendlier to Roman authority than the Pharisees. But it was the Pharisees that Jesus had the most negative interactions with, presumably because He directly attacked *their* adherence to *oral traditions.*

"You have a fine way of setting aside the commands of God in order to observe your own traditions!" **Mark 7:9** (NIV)

Because they were more concerned with politics than religion, the Sadducees *ignored* Jesus. It was not until the problem literally appeared on their doorstep in Jerusalem and jeopardized the *status quo*, that they finally acknowledged the threat.

By this time in his ministry, Jesus was well known throughout the region. There had already been several attempts at arresting Him along with three assassination attempts. So they already deemed him to be a threat.

They concluded that if Jesus were allowed to continue performing His signs, it would cause the people to turn away from them and they would lose control. Once that happened, they believed the Romans would view this as a threat and that they would act aggressively to put it down, even to the point of destroying the Temple and, along with it, the nation of Israel.

The fear of unwanted Roman intrusion into their affairs caused the Sadducees to lay down their philosophical differences with the Pharisees and concentrate on this common enemy. For their part, the Pharisees recognized that Jesus was a dangerous person. He had continually bested them in all public debate and the people were declaring Him as more than just a man. More importantly, Jesus did not deny this.

Once the two parties united, they set into motion a plan to get rid of the *Jesus problem.*

Prior to His arrival in Jerusalem, for the Passover, He had been to Bethany. It was there where He performed the miracle of raising His friend Lazarus from the dead. The Bible reports that many Jews, who had come to pay their respects to the dead man's sister, Mary, witnessed this act. When they saw this, many believed in Jesus, but some of them went to the Pharisees and told them what Jesus had done.

There are over thirty recorded instances of Jesus performing public miracles witnessed by a multitude of people, none of which, including religious leaders, denied they occurred. Instead, the religious leaders accused Him of being able to perform these acts through the power of the devil.

But when the Pharisees heard it, they said, 'This fellow doth not cast out devils, but by Beelzebub the prince of the devils.' **Matthew 12:22-24** (KJV)

It should be noted that, while the story of Lazarus seems to end, it doesn't. According to the Eastern Orthodox Church, Lazarus lived for another thirty years after he was raised from the dead.

Sometime after the Resurrection of Christ, Lazarus was forced to flee Judea because of rumored plots on his life and went to Cyprus, where he was appointed by Paul and Barnabas as the first bishop of Kition (present day Larnaca). So it is extremely unlikely that such a public person would have been the subject of a resurrection hoax.

It was at this point that the chief priests and the Pharisees called a meeting of the Sanhedrin to address the issue. Caiaphas, who was the high priest, made the fateful declaration that it was *better that one man should die than a whole nation should perish*. The order went out that if anyone knew where Jesus was they should report it, so they could arrest Him.

When Jesus arrived in Jerusalem, He was greeted by adoring crowds. While it most likely annoyed the Sanhedrin, they probably realized that seizing Him at that moment would have only created more problems than it would have solved. That reluctance changed after Monday, when Jesus appeared at the temple to teach and found the courtyard filled with vendors.

To understand the significance of this event, you must first understand what the temple market meant to the religious authority. While estimates on the general population of Jerusalem vary, the number of pilgrims attending the Passover could very well have tripled or quadrupled it. The courtyard of the temple would have served as a thriving commercial environment, catering to the needs of these pilgrims in the form of livestock merchants, who provided animals for sacrifice, as well as money changer tables, where they could exchange Greek and Roman money for Jewish and Tyrian funds. This was a highly lucrative business and, while they reserved part of the profit for the temple treasury, a considerable amount also made its way into the private coffers of the priests.

On Monday morning, Jesus appeared at the temple and began to teach. However, His sermon was interrupted by an argument involving the money changers, as well the raucous movement of livestock through the courtyard. Jesus stepped down from where He had been teaching and within minutes He had cleared out the grounds of the merchants and money changers. A nearby group of Roman soldiers had responded to the *disturbance*, but upon their arrival, order had already been restored and the crowd was now quiet. Still, in an attempt to maintain the peace, a guard was placed at the temple and nothing could be brought inside, which effectively ended all commercial business.

On Tuesday evening a fateful meeting of the Sanhedrin was called to order and they decreed the death of Jesus. Orders were issued to bring Him before the high Jewish court before midnight on Thursday, but with instructions that they must not take him into custody in public, for fear of an uprising.

Judas Iscariot, the apostle who would ultimately betray Jesus, believed that they could apprehend Him quietly at the home of John Mark, but when they arrived, they found that He had already departed. Judas' plan had been to take custody of Jesus when he knew that there was little chance of resistance. Of the eleven Apostles that would have been with Him, he knew that only Simon Peter and Simon Zelotes were armed with swords. However, if they attempted to take Him at their camp, the number of followers would have grown and Judas also knew that they would have access to additional weapons, as Simon Zelotes had an ample store of arms in his possession.

Judas returned to the temple where the priests had begun to gather and advised them of what had happened. He informed them they would need more guards, more than the temple could provide. A request was then made directly to Pontius Pilate to provide the adequate number of soldiers. This is historically significant, because it elevates the matter from a strictly religious one, to one requiring official government intervention.

Initially, Pilate wanted nothing to do with the matter, but since the presiding officer of the Sanhedrin was making the request for this assistance, the governor felt compelled to grant it. He reasoned that if there was any impropriety, he could correct it later.

When Judas arrived at the Garden of Gethsemane he was accompanied by more than sixty temple guards, Roman soldiers, and representatives of the temple. After seizing Jesus, they brought Him before the council for trial.

Normally, the court proceeded with due caution, when trying someone on a capital charge, but nothing about this proceeding was normal. The reality was that they had already determined Jesus' fate and were now looking for the evidence to justify that finding. Caiaphas was more of a prosecuting attorney than an unbiased jurist.

After two meetings of the court, they had drawn up an indictment, which was to be presented to Pilate, ordering him to be put Jesus to death.

The charges facing him were:

1. He had deceived the people of the Jewish nation and incited them to rebellion.

2. He had instructed the Jewish people not to pay tribute to Caesar.

3. By claiming to be a king, and founder of a new kingdom, he incited treason against the emperor.

When Jesus was brought before Pilate, he faced a dilemma. Pilate did not get along with the Jews. Of all the Roman provinces, Judea was the most difficult to govern and he had already made a number of missteps along the way. As a result, he had what could best be described as a *precarious* relationship with the Jews.

For their part, Jewish leaders knew that Pilate feared for his position before Tiberius, and they skillfully used this knowledge against him. Pilate made the grave mistake of capitulating to them. Once they understood his weakness in making threats which he feared to execute, they used it to their advantage.

While interviewing Jesus, Pilate's fundamental question was whether He considered himself to be the King of the Jews. This was done in an attempt to determine if He actually posed any political threat to the Empire. But when Pilate asked him: "*Are you the king of the Jews?*" Jesus' reply was only, "*Thou sayest it.*" Absent a confession, Pilate felt it was not enough for Him to be seen as a legitimate political threat and not one worthy of capital punishment.

After interviewing Jesus, Pilate found no evidence of the charges against Him and informed the crowd of Jews of his findings. One of the Sanhedrin came forth and claimed that Jesus' had been stirring up the people, first in Galilee and now here. When Pilate heard them say that Jesus had begun in Galilee, he saw it as a chance to rid himself of the decision and had Jesus sent to King Herod.

When Jesus appeared before Herod, the Jews voiced their accusations against Him, but when Herod asked Jesus about them He refused to answer. Herod was overly cautious about taking any action against Jesus, especially after he'd had John the Baptist killed. Jesus' silence left Herod with no legal recourse, and, since he had no jurisdiction on activities in Judea, he sent Him back to Pilate.

The return of Jesus put Pilate in a tough position. He had already stated that he had found no evidence to convict. Likewise, Herod had obviously reached the same conclusion, but the assembled mob still called for Jesus' death.

It had become customary at that time to issue a pardon to a convicted or condemned person in honor of the Passover feast. Pilate reasoned that, since Jesus had been a popular preacher among the people, that he might extricate himself from this quandary by pardoning Jesus. However, a call went out from the crowd to release a prisoner called Barabbas instead. Barabbas had been apprehended in the act of robbery and murder on the Jericho road, but he was also the son of a priest. The crowd's rejection of Jesus, in favor of the convicted murderer, stunned Pilate.

It should also be mentioned that Pilate's wife, Claudia Procula, who was a partial convert to Judaism and who later became a Christian, sent a note to her husband advising him not to become involved with the case that had been brought before him. The note allegedly read: "*I pray you have nothing to do with this innocent and just man whom they call Jesus. I have suffered many things in a dream this night because of him.*"

As the crowd became more raucous in their calls to release Barabbas and crucify Jesus, Pilate became more cautious. If he had been a just man, he would have acquitted Jesus outright and released Him, but his fears of a Jewish revolt, and the potential damage to his own political career, overruled his moral compass.

In one last ditch appeal, Pilate ordered the soldiers to remove Jesus to the courtyard of the praetorium where He would be scourged.

We should note that this decision was actually an illegal procedure by Pilate. Under Roman law, only those condemned to death by crucifixion would be subject to scourging. It was a heinous and brutal act designed to bring a convicted person to a state just short of collapse or death. The only people exempt from this barbaric act were women, Roman senators, and Roman soldiers, except those found guilty of desertion.

I believe there are no words to describe the sheer brutality of scourging, but perhaps it will serve to describe the instruments used to administer the punishment to the convicted. The device used was called a Roman *flagrum*. It is a short whip which comprised several leather thongs, of varying lengths, which had small iron balls and sharp pieces of bone tied at different intervals.

The convicted person would be stripped of his clothing and his hands would be tied to an upright post. As the soldiers administered the scourging, the iron balls would inflict excruciatingly painful bruises while the leather thongs and sharpened bone would lacerate the skin and underlying tissue. With each lash of the whip, the device would dig deeper and deeper, until it tore into the skeletal muscle, resulting in ever increasing blood loss.

Under Jewish law, there was a limit of thirty-nine lashes imposed, but these were Roman soldiers and they were under no such numerical limitation. Their only consideration was limiting their punishment to the point the convicted could still be crucified.

If you are inclined to see an accurate visual representation of this punishment, then I would recommend a viewing of the movie, **The Passion of Christ**, by Mel Gibson.

Pilate's original belief was that, by administering this severe punishment to Jesus, he could appeal to the gathered crowd to accept the scourging as being sufficient for the charge of blasphemy, but when he produced Jesus before the crowd they shouted, "Crucify him."

Despite knowing that Jesus was innocent, Pilate agreed to the crowds demand, but before he did this, he had a basin of water produced and washed his hands, declaring to the mob, "*I am innocent of this man's blood. It is your responsibility!*"

It was customary that a sign, relating the name and charges of the condemned, be affixed to the cross. Pilate had a sign written that read: "*Jesus of Nazareth, the king of the Jews.*" This incensed the Jewish authorities, who demanded that it be removed or at least amended to read "*He said, 'I am the king of the Jews,'*" but Pilate refused.

Then Jesus was taken to *Golgotha*, the place of the skull, and crucified.

Standing vigil at the cross were a number of people including Mary, Jesus' mother, John (the disciple whom he loved), Mary, the wife of Clopas and sister of Jesus' mother, Salome, and Mary Magdalene. Also present were the soldiers and centurion, the chief priests, members of the Sanhedrin, as well as onlookers from the surrounding country, and they all *witnessed* the death of Jesus.

And that is precisely where Christianity should have ended, but it didn't.

So, at this point in the investigation we know four specific things:

1. Jesus lived.
2. He was deemed a viable threat by the authorities.
3. He was taken into custody.
4. He was sentenced to death.

CHAPTER EIGHT
(Life after Death)

The next day, the one after Preparation Day, the chief priests and the Pharisees went to Pilate. "Sir," they said, "we remember that while he was still alive that deceiver said, 'After three days I will rise again.' So give the order for the tomb to be made secure until the third day. Otherwise, his disciples may come and steal the body and tell the people that he has been raised from the dead. This last deception will be worse than the first." "Take a guard," Pilate answered. "Go, make the tomb as secure as you know how." So they went and made the tomb secure by putting a seal on the stone and posting the guard. **Matthew 27: 62-66** (NIV)

So, at this point, we have established that Jesus was convicted, sentenced to death, and that punishment has been meted out.

Before we address the topic of resurrection, we must first consider claims by some who have argued that it was customary procedure for the Romans to leave crucified criminals hanging from their *tree*. Their argument is that since they would have left Jesus on the cross, he couldn't have risen from the grave three days later. This is where understanding history comes into play.

I won't deny that it was a common practice to leave crucified criminals in plain view, which served as a visual deterrent to others, but again we must look deeper into the issue. While this certainly happened in most areas of the Roman Empire, it was not an ironclad rule. Remember, this is Jerusalem and, for all his issues, Jesus' was still a Jew and this was occurring at Passover. Something Pilate would have been keenly aware of, especially with the influx of pilgrims to Jerusalem.

Jewish law is very clear on this matter: *"And if a man have committed a sin worthy of death, and he be put to death, and thou hang him on a tree: His body shall not remain all night upon the tree, but thou shalt in any wise bury him that day; (for he that is hanged is accursed of God;) that thy land be not defiled, which the LORD thy God giveth thee for an inheritance."* **Deuteronomy 21:22-23** (KJV)

Others cite the example of when Romans crucified thousands of Jews during the Jewish Rebellion in AD 70 and left the corpses to rot on their crosses. Of course that is also true, but that is only one example and that was during a period of war. Many rules go out the window under these conditions, but Jerusalem was not in a period of war during Jesus' crucifixion. Quite the contrary, it was a period of relative calm in Judea. So there would have been no reason to rile up the populace, especially at Passover, by violating such a significant law.

In addition to this, Roman law also stipulated that, if requested, they should release the remains of the dead for the purpose of burial. So when Joseph of Arimathea, a wealthy man and a member of the council, sought Pilate's permission to bury the body in his personal sepulcher. It would have been perfectly normal for Pilate to grant the request.

But Jewish leaders knew of the continued theological threat to them, which Jesus had posed in life, and they were not about to take any chances in death. They were aware of His audacious prediction that, *"The Son of Man must be delivered over to the hands of sinners, be crucified and on the third day be raised again."* **Luke 24:7** (NIV)

They feared that His followers would try to remove the body, in order to further that claim, so they appealed to Pilate to provide a military contingent in order to prevent this and he agreed. These men were not from the temple guard, they were regular Roman soldiers. After they sealed the tomb, they would have stood guard in four-hour shifts. Having received their order to protect the tomb, they knew that they would face their own death if they allowed anything to happen.

When the soldiers arrived, they would have taken stock of the situation and determined that the body of Jesus was inside. The tomb was brand new and had been cut out of solid rock. Since it was new, there were no other bodies present that would have caused any *confusion*. They put the large rock stone in place and affixed a seal. The seal was significant. Like the police seals I once put on locations, this was a visible sign that the tomb was under the power and control of the Roman authorities.

Violating this seal today would result in a criminal charge, but a violation of the seal then would result in the *death* of the offender. Of course, in order to even violate the seal, they would first have had to get past the Roman soldiers.

Now, there are several competing arguments that exist over this point, including some allegations that there were no guards and that the Gospel of Matthew is a lie, but upon closer examination, this doesn't make sense.

Consider that immediately following the proclamation that Jesus had risen from the grave, the Jewish polemic claimed that that the disciples *stole* the body. The Christian response was that this would have been impossible, since there was a Roman guard posted at the tomb. At this moment, we should pause and realize that both sides now concede that they had placed the body of Jesus inside the tomb and it was now *empty*. If the Christian claim that there were Roman soldiers guarding it was untrue, the Jewish authorities could have easily dismissed it, but it wasn't. Instead they upped the ante and made the audacious claim that the guards were there, but were remiss in their duties and had fallen asleep.

Why this gets glossed over by most people amazes me, but I think it speaks volumes as to the lack of historical knowledge we have concerning the Roman Empire.

For context, we need to understand that the history of Rome begins with the Roman Kingdom in 753 BC continues through the Roman Republic from 509 to 27 BC and ends with the fall of the western Roman Empire in AD 1453. At its height, in AD 117, the Empire stretched from England and Spain in the west to Persia in the east. Rome did not achieve this dominance, nor survive for over two thousand years, with an incompetent military force.

There are countless stories, provided by Roman historians, which provide us with clear insight as to how the Roman army operated. It is worth pointing out that death was a very common solution to any number of perceived deficiencies, including sleeping while on guard duty. In addition, punishment was not limited to the offending soldier, but could also be applied to the offending soldier's unit in a practice known as *decimation*.

The Roman historian *Polybius* provides us with one of the most thorough accounts of Roman military discipline, including that of the night watch, and the consequences of any failure. The following provides insight into what discipline the guards at Jesus' tomb would have faced.

"When this time comes, the man to whom the first watch fell by lot makes his rounds accompanied by some friends as witnesses. He visits the posts mentioned in his orders, not only those near the vallum and the gates, but the pickets also of the infantry maniples and cavalry squadrons. If he finds the guards of the first watch awake he receives their tesserae (a small token), but if he finds that anyone is asleep or has left his post, he calls those with him to witness the fact, and proceeds on his rounds. Those who go the rounds in the succeeding watches act in a similar manner. As I said, the charge of sounding a bugle at the beginning of each watch, so that those going the rounds may visit the different stations at the right time, falls on the centurions of the first maniple of the triarii in each legion, who take it by turns for a day."

"Each of the men who have gone the rounds brings back the tesserae at daybreak to the tribune. If they deliver them all they are suffered to depart without question; but if one of them delivers fewer than the number of stations visited, they find out from examining the signs on the tesserae which station is missing, and on ascertaining this the tribune calls the centurion of the maniple and he brings before him the men who were on picket duty, and they are confronted with the patrol. If the fault is that of the picket, the patrol makes matters clear at once by calling the men who had

accompanied him, for he is bound to do this; but if nothing of the kind has happened, the fault rests on him. A court-martial composed of all the tribunes at once meets to try him, and if he is found guilty he is punished by the bastinado. This is inflicted as follows: The tribune takes a cudgel and just touches the condemned man with it, after which all in the camp beat or stone him, in most cases dispatching him in the camp itself. But even those who manage to escape are not saved thereby. For they are not allowed to return to their homes and none of the family would dare to receive such a man in his house; so that those who have of course fallen into this misfortune are utterly ruined. The same punishment is inflicted on the optio and on the praefect of the squadron, if they do not give the proper orders at the right time to the patrols and the praefect of the next squadron. Thus, owing to the extreme severity and inevitableness of the penalty, the night watches of the Roman army are most scrupulously kept."

Military duty and discipline were serious matters in those days and punishment for failure was both harsh and swift. So the idea that the soldiers assigned to guard the tomb of Jesus would fall asleep or desert their post, without any punishment, is beyond the pale. For all of Pilate's faults in dealing with the Jews, he was still a harsh man who would have taken immediate action in dealing with his subordinates.

Given the gravity of this highly charged situation, coupled with the uneasy alliance with the Romans, it is unlikely that the Jewish authority would have left this matter alone to the Romans. We can safely assume that they may have also left several people behind to act as witnesses to the soldiers. Either way, there is a powerful argument that neither group was the least bit supportive of Jesus or of His followers.

Yet on Easter morning, when Mary Magdalene, Mary, the mother of James, and Salome, arrived at the tomb to carry out their final devotion to Jesus, by anointing His body with spices and oils, they find the tomb empty and the soldiers gone. This is a very important moment, because we must stop and consider that these women went there for a *purpose*. They were doing a solemn duty and they fully expected Jesus' body to be there. When they find the stone removed from the tomb, their first assumption is that someone had stolen the body.

Now Mary stood outside the tomb crying. As she wept, she bent over to look into the tomb and saw two angels in white, seated where Jesus' body had been, one at the head and the other at the foot. They asked her, "Woman, why are you crying?" "They have taken my Lord away," she said, "and I don't know where they have put him." At this, she turned around and saw Jesus standing there, but she did not realize that it was Jesus. He asked her, "Woman, why are you crying? Who is it you are looking for?" Thinking he was the gardener, she said, "Sir, if you have carried him away, tell me where you have put him, and I will get him." **John 20: 11-15** (NIV)

At this juncture, it is important that we take pause and consider the totality of what has just happened.

Jesus, who triumphantly arrived in Jerusalem only a few days earlier to raucous cheers, was arrested on trumped-up charges, grotesquely beaten, and then hung on a cross to die a painful death. We know that a multitude of people witnessed His death, and that His body is now missing.

So ask yourself this question: *Where are the apostles?*

For three years these twelve men, who we know as: **Peter** (born Simon), **Andrew**, brother of Peter, **James**, son of Zebedee, **John**, brother of James, son of Zebedee, **Philip**, **Bartholomew**, **Thomas**, **Matthew**, **James**, son of Alphaeus, **Judas Thaddeus**, also known as Jude, **Simon** the Zealot, also known as Simon the Canaanite, and **Judas Iscariot**, accompanied Jesus in His ministry from Capernaum to Jerusalem. They each gave up their lives and careers to travel with Him.

Now we all know what happened regarding Judas Iscariot, who betrayed Jesus to the Sanhedrin, but where are the others?

Here is where my investigative bells and whistles go off.

I have investigated hundreds of cases over the years and conducted even more interviews and interrogations. The moment I responded to a scene one of my initial questions was always, *"Where are the witnesses?"*

Well, at this moment they are in hiding.

Now the apostles are just the core group. We know that Judas Iscariot expressed concern about apprehending Jesus in the open, because he feared that the number of followers with Him could be threefold the number of apostles. This means that there were potentially a lot of folks that may have been involved, but for the purpose of this investigation we will only concentrate on the apostles and some immediate disciples.

Immediately following Jesus' arrest in the Garden of Gethsemane, the majority of apostles scatter in the wind. Of the eleven, they document only John as being at both the trial and the crucifixion. Peter, arguably the staunchest of Jesus' supporters, attempted to monitor the situation from the periphery, but it's not long until they confront him about his association with Jesus and he disappears from the scene.

This tells me something very important. There is only one reason you go into hiding after a homicide occurs and that is because you fear that you will be the next victim!

As I examined the case, I understood why this would be a very realistic concern to the assembled group. They knew that one of their own had already betrayed them and the murder of their leader showed that the Jewish authority took the threat seriously. It was clear that the Romans also had a vested interest in quashing any further religious *issues* that threatened their authority.

In order to appreciate the mindset of the apostles now, we must take a step back in time. As Shakespeare once wrote, *"What's past is prologue,"* holds true for the apostles.

Jesus spent the first thirty years of His life as a simple carpenter, from the small village of Galilee, before emerging onto the scene from relative obscurity. He had no formal religious training, yet He possessed an inherent ability to teach with absolute authority. Jesus was also able to connect with people on an intimate level, and not just with the socially acceptable *good* people.

Jesus hung out with the *outcasts* of society. Repeatedly we are shown examples of this. Whether it was a prostitute, a tax collector, or a leper, He sought those who had been forsaken by mainstream religion.

"When the teachers of the law who were Pharisees saw him eating with the sinners and tax collectors, they asked his disciples: 'Why does he eat with tax collectors and sinners?' On hearing this, Jesus said to them, 'It is not the healthy who need a doctor, but the sick. I have not come to call the righteous, but sinners.'" **Mark 2: 16-17** (NIV)

This fanned the flames of anger and resentment among the religious authorities, which followed Him throughout His ministry, but it also secured a following among the common people, including the apostles.

Unfortunately, a lot of Jesus' messages were lost on these people, including amongst His followers. In many ways they misunderstood the role that Jesus was fulfilling, because they had their preconceived idea of what they thought was going to happen. They believed that Jesus was the promised Messiah. Under Abrahamic Law they saw Him as the *Son of David*, a savior. He was the promised one, the *conquering king*, who had come to liberate them from the oppressive yoke they were under and would unite the tribes of Israel. They were so caught up in what they had been *taught* that they had a hard time *listening* to what Jesus was saying to them, and this was especially true for His closest followers.

Consider Jesus' statement to the apostles at the last supper: *"Where I am going, you cannot follow now, but you will follow later."* To which Peter replies: *"Lord, why can't I follow you now? I will lay down my life for you."* **John 10: 36-37** (NIV)

Even after three years, they still didn't understand what Jesus' mission was. They believed that He was going to launch a *physically* rebellion and conquer the establishment. It seems the message of Isaiah, written hundreds of years before Jesus' birth, had been lost.

"Who has believed our message and to whom has the arm of the Lord been revealed? He grew up before him like a tender shoot, and like a root out of dry ground. He had no beauty or majesty to attract us to him, nothing in his appearance that we should desire him. He was despised and rejected by mankind, a man of suffering, and familiar with pain. Like one from whom people hide their faces he was despised, and we held him in low esteem. Surely he took up our pain and bore our suffering, yet we considered him punished by God, stricken by him, and afflicted. But he was pierced for our transgressions, he was crushed for our iniquities; the punishment that brought us peace was on him, and by his wounds we are healed. We all, like sheep, have gone astray, each of us has turned to our own way; and the Lord has laid on him the iniquity of us all. He was oppressed and afflicted, yet he did not open his mouth; he was led like a lamb to the slaughter, and as a sheep before its shearers is silent, so he did not open his mouth. By oppression and judgment he was taken away. Yet who of his generation protested? For he was cut off from the land of the living; for the transgression of my people he was punished. He was assigned a grave with the wicked and with the rich in his death, though he had done no violence, nor was any deceit in his mouth. Yet it was the Lord's will to crush him and cause him to suffer, and though the Lord makes his life an offering for sin, he will see his offspring and prolong his days, and the will of the Lord will prosper in his hand. After he has suffered, he will see the light of life and be satisfied; by his knowledge my righteous servant will justify many, and he will bear their iniquities. Therefore I will give him a portion among the great, and he will divide the spoils with the strong, because he poured out his life

unto death, and was numbered with the transgressors. For he bore the sin of many, and made intercession for the transgressors." **Isaiah 53: 1-12** (NIV)

So it isn't difficult to imagine the chaos that ensued after Jesus' arrest, torture, and crucifixion. We only have to look at Peter's actions, after Jesus' arrest, to understand the prevailing mindset. At the point of Peter denying that he was a follower, Jesus was *still alive*. The worst was yet to come, but the very moment things went bad, even the closest distanced themselves from Him.

It reminds me of the old saying, *"With friends like these, who needs enemies?"*

The remaining eleven apostles were the followers and they knew they had murdered their leader for what He was preaching. That they might be next would have surely weighed heavy upon them.

Many people will risk their life for something they believe in, but few will risk it for something they know to be an outright lie. That their first action was to immediately go into hiding reinforces a key component of nature: the need for self-preservation.

Each of them believed that Jesus was the Messiah and they believed that He would be victorious. So when He died, that belief died with Him. There was no victory, there was no *smiting of foes*, and there was no triumphant king sitting on his throne. There was just a bloody and horrifically beaten corpse placed inside a tomb.

Despite what they might have felt in their *heart*, this was something tangible, something visceral, and their *brains* couldn't deny it. They had witnessed firsthand the full weight of the Roman government, coupled with the religious authorities, come down and destroy their fledgling movement.

Now they were just waiting for the knock on the door that would usher in their own demise.

While it might seem counterintuitive today, given what Jesus preached about His death and resurrection, to the apostles who lived through His death it would seem inconceivable.

I have had people ask me, "*Yes, but what about the things they (the apostles) witnessed, all the miracles, the healing, and the raising of Lazarus from the dead? Surely they would have believed in Jesus' power.*"

I agree.

As witnesses to these events, they would have surely believed that Jesus had been imbued with some type of divine power. Even among the religious leaders it was believed that Jesus possessed some supernatural power, although they ascribed this to *satanic origins.* But we must also remember that the apostles would have also seen that, despite what He had done for others, He still was unable to save Himself, which most likely would have frightened them even more. If this man, who raised the dead, could not protect Himself, then what chance would they have?

So when Mary and the other women arrive back at the house, to tell them what they had witnessed, we see that the apostles are confused and don't believe them. Even after they inspect the tomb, and find only Jesus' burial linen, they still do not accept it.

It will take something truly amazing, something miraculous, to change their way of thinking and that is precisely what happens.

Over the course of the next forty days, the risen Christ is witnessed by a multitude of people. The Bible lists the following events:

- Sunday Morning: Witnessed by women at tomb

- Sunday Afternoon: Witnessed by Simon Peter

- Sunday Afternoon: Witnessed by two disciples on the road to Emmaus (Cleopas is named)

- Sunday Night: Witnessed by ten of the apostles

- 1 Week Later: Witnessed by all the apostles (*the Doubting Thomas incident*)

- Within 40 days: Witnessed by seven of the apostles in Galilee

- Within 40 days: Witnessed by all the apostles (*the Great Commission*)

- Within 40 days: Witnessed by five hundred people

- Within 40 days: Witnessed by James (half-brother of Jesus)

- Beyond 40 days: Witnessed by Paul (Saul of Tarsus)

I have heard several explanations offered for the multiple post-crucifixion appearances of Jesus. They range from hallucinations, mistaken identity, lying, or a faked death. But when you consider each of them at face value, they seem to hold inconsiderable weight.

With *hallucinations*, I could see it afflicting one person, or even a small group, but when you factor in the multiple sightings, at multiple locations, by a large and diverse group of people, than I think you can dismiss this claim.

The same thing applies to the *mistaken identity* claim. There were too many people who knew Jesus intimately. We can find the strongest argument in the appearance before James. Say what you will, but your sibling will know who you are.

Jesus faked his own death. Again, this theory only holds water if you completely discount everything we know about the Roman military. Reluctantly or not, Pilate handed Jesus over to be scourged and then crucified. Under Roman law, if a soldier let a prisoner, who had been sentenced to death, escape, then the soldier was executed in his place. We also know that Pilate only gave the body up to Joseph *after* they informed him that Jesus was dead. Even the Jewish authorities acknowledged His death.

Also, engaging in deception would have been fundamentally inconsistent with Jesus' reputation for being honest and truthful. These were character traits that even His enemies openly recognized.

In **Matthew 22:16-21**, we are told that the disciples of the Pharisees stated: "We know you are a *man of integrity* and that you *teach the way of God in accordance with the truth.*" (NIV)

Some contend that the disciples were simply *lying* about it all. It would be convenient to chalk this all up to some elaborate hoax, but then the obvious question arises: *Why?*

Now, for those inclined to believe the Bible is a fictional account, I would ask that you consider the following:

- 1 Corinthians was written around AD 53-57

- The Gospel of Mark was written around AD 66-70

- Acts was written around AD 80-90

- The Gospel of Matthew was written around AD 86-90

- The Gospel of Luke was written around AD 86-90

- The Gospel of John was written around AD 95-110

The significance of these books is that they document the life, death, and resurrection of Jesus Christ generally within one generation's time. Remember, Christ died around AD 33. This means that the authors were referencing specific events and that the majority of people living in these areas were still *alive* and could be questioned about the details.

Paul wrote his letter to the Corinthians within two decades of the crucifixion. In it, Paul makes statements to people whom he knew could easily investigate the truthfulness of his claim. He goes even further and specifically tells them that over five hundred brothers, "*most of whom are still alive,*" witnessed the risen Christ. That is a heck of a bold statement if you are engaged in a hoax.

We should also understand something very significant about what the apostles were preaching. The method of Jesus' death made the spread of Christianity impossible.

They considered death by crucifixion an *obscene* form of torture and it was a punishment reserved for the most heinous and despised criminals. It was intended to send a powerful message to witnesses that they should not engage in any similar activity as the crucified person. Death was slow, excruciating (from the Latin *ex crucio*, meaning "out of crucifying"), gruesome, humiliating, and public. Among Romans, they considered death by crucifixion to be the ultimate dishonor. So much so that suicide was a more respectable alternative. Those hearing the message that the *Son of God* had died by *crucifixion* would have found it incredulous, and the apostles knew this.

Another important historical aspect, which many people fail to consider, is that Jesus' followers were all first century Jews. The reason this takes on significance is that, during this period of time, women held a very low social status. They were often illiterate and considered *untrustworthy.* Women were not even permitted to testify in legal proceedings. It is a point made, but often overlooked, in **Luke 24:11**, when the women say they had seen Jesus and the disciples discounted it as "*nonsense*" and "*did not believe the women.*" So it is highly unlikely that, given this fact, the writer's would have chosen women to be the very *first eyewitnesses* to a hoax.

But for this to have all been some elaborate ploy, there would have had to have been an *end game*, something that would have benefited the group. Yet when we examine the mission of Jesus, it leaves us with very little in the form of personal gain.

There is a proverb that says, "*The road to hell is paved with good intentions.*" It is a saying which is unfortunately very true with many religious and charitable organizations. What starts out as an excellent idea, like helping the poor, sometimes becomes a path to personal enrichment, under the guise of *operating costs*. Things were no different during the time of Jesus, and we already know that His behavior at the temple, in chasing out the money changers, was a crucial factor that led to His death.

So what was in it for Jesus or the apostles?

Well, the simple truth is there was nothing to be gained, at least not in this life.

While Jesus Christ was *the* most important individual to walk the face of the earth, the Bible reveals that the gospel Jesus brought was *not* about Himself. Everything Jesus taught was about the *Kingdom of God*. He never elevated Himself above the Father, never called for any to worship Him. In fact, we can sum up Jesus' entire ministry in one statement:

"Love the Lord your God with all your heart and with all your soul and with all your mind. This is the first and greatest commandment. And the second is like it: Love your neighbor as yourself. All the Law and the Prophets hang on these two commandments." **Mark 25: 37-4** (NIV)

Everything we read about in the Bible eschews personal gain.

In the case of the man who asked Jesus how he could get eternal life, Jesus told him, *"If you want to be perfect, go, sell your possessions and give to the poor, and you will have treasure in heaven. Then come, follow me."* **Mark 19:21** (NIV)

Jesus didn't say donate your wealth to Me, He said donate to the poor and *then* follow Me.

When we examine the life of the apostles, we see this same theme continued. If they knew the story of the risen Christ was a lie, they sure didn't act like it.

Taking a closer look at the life of the apostles, immediately following the crucifixion, we see exactly what we should see: *Men in fear for their very lives.* This is human nature at work. Yet within a very brief period of time, the timid lambs have become evangelical lions.

The greatest case for Jesus' resurrection is the behavior of the apostles.

Before Jesus ascended into Heaven, He gave His apostles the *Great Commission*, telling them that they should, *"Go, therefore, and make disciples of all nations."* Having been assigned the divine mandate to travel the world for the sake of the Gospel, the apostles didn't waste their time.

These men were so convinced of Jesus' resurrection that they were willing to endure ongoing persecution and imprisonment for preaching the case of the resurrected Christ. Make no mistake about it, these men knew full well what the Jewish authorities and Roman government had done to Jesus. His crucifixion sent an obvious message that any threat to their way of life would be dealt with quickly and with extreme prejudice.

If what these men were preaching was *not* true, then they were lying and were unexplainably willing to suffer great persecution and martyrdom for something they knew to be a hoax.

Instead of being afraid to be seen or even identified as a follower of Jesus, the remaining eleven disciples began preaching that He had been raised from the dead. These statements were not made behind closed doors, or in dark alleyways, but publicly in the very same city where Jesus had been put to death as a political traitor and religious blasphemer.

To put this in better perspective, on the first Pentecost, a mere seven weeks after the crucifixion, the apostle Peter gave a sermon to thousands in Jerusalem attesting to the resurrection of Jesus. There is no doubt that everyone in Jerusalem knew what had happened.

His next sermon was at the Jewish temple a few days later where he boldly proclaimed to the assembled congregation, "*The God of Abraham, Isaac and Jacob, the God of our fathers, has glorified his servant Jesus. You handed him over to be killed, and you disowned him before Pilate, though he had decided to let him go. You disowned the Holy and Righteous One and asked that a murderer be released to you. You killed the author of life, but God raised him from the dead. We are witnesses of this.*" **Acts 3:13-15** (NIV)

Acts 4, provides us another example, where Peter and John were preaching at the temple, and Peter had healed a lame beggar. Immediately they are confronted by the religious leaders.

The priests and the captain of the temple guard and the Sadducees came up to Peter and John while they were speaking to the people. They were greatly disturbed because the apostles were teaching the people, proclaiming in Jesus the resurrection of the dead. They seized Peter and John and, because it was evening, they put them in jail until the next day. But many who heard the message believed; so the number of men who believed grew to about five thousand.

The next day the rulers, the elders and the teachers of the law met in Jerusalem. Annas the high priest was there, and so were Caiaphas, John, Alexander and others of the high priest's family. They had Peter and John brought before them and began to question them: "By what power or what name did you do this?"

Then Peter, filled with the Holy Spirit, said to them: "Rulers and elders of the people! If we are being called to account today for an act of kindness shown to a man who was lame and are being asked how he was healed, then know this, you and all the people of Israel: It is by the name of Jesus Christ of Nazareth, whom you crucified but whom God raised from the dead, that this man stands before you healed. Jesus is 'the stone you builders rejected, which has become the cornerstone.' Salvation is found in no one else, for there is no other name under heaven given to mankind by which we must be saved."

When they saw the courage of Peter and John and realized that they were unschooled, ordinary men, they were astonished and they took note that these men had been with Jesus. But since they could see the man who had been healed standing there with them, there was nothing they could say. So they ordered them to withdraw from the Sanhedrin and then conferred together. "What are we going to do with these men?" they asked. "Everyone living in Jerusalem knows they have performed a notable sign, and we cannot deny it. But to stop this thing from spreading any further among the people, we must warn them to speak no longer to anyone in this name."

Then they called them in again and commanded them not to speak or teach at all in the name of Jesus. But Peter and John replied, "Which is right in God's eyes: to listen to you, or to him? You be the judges! As for us, we cannot help speaking about what we have seen and heard." **Acts 4:1-20** (NIV)

Again, the Book of Acts was written shortly after these activities occurred and during a time when there would have been numerous witnesses to the event. The religious leaders involved were the same ones who had orchestrated Jesus' death, so Peter and John knew exactly who they were dealing with. The animus towards Christianity did not die with Jesus. There was a massive persecution of Christians orchestrated by the Jewish and Roman authorities. So the apostles would have understood that their preaching would mostly likely result in their own deaths, yet they refused to capitulate.

And die they did.

"Remember what I told you: 'A servant is not greater than his master.' If they persecuted me, they will persecute you also." **John 15:20** (NIV)

All but one of the eleven original disciples died a martyr, yet not one of them ever abandoned their faith. An examination of the lives of the disciples gives us an idea of just how much they were willing to sacrifice, in order to preach the Gospel.

Peter – Founded the church at Antioch and is credited, along with Paul, of founding the church in Rome. Tradition says that by Emperor Nero ordered his execution and that nailed him to the cross. Peter requested that his head be placed toward the ground with his feet raised up, keeping with his belief that he was not worthy of crucifixion in the same manner as his Lord.

Andrew – Is considered the founder and the first bishop of the Church of Byzantium. He spread the Gospel from Greece to what is modern day Russia. Tradition holds that he was martyred in the Greek city of Patras by Aegaeas, the governor of Edessa, in the name of the Roman senate, after he had converted the governor's wife to Christianity. He was crucified on an X-shaped cross, at his own request, as he also deemed himself unworthy to die on the same type of cross as Jesus.

James the Great – Preached in Judea and was beheaded by the sword at the authority of King Herod (Herod Agrippa). He is the only apostle whose death is specifically documented in the New Testament, leading many to believe that he was the first to be martyred for his faith.

John – Is the brother of James the Great and the author of several books in the New Testament, including the Gospel of John and Revelation. He founded the churches of Smyrna, Pergamos, Sardis, Philadelphia, Laodicea, and Thyatira. When Domitian succeeded Nero as Emperor, he began a crusade against the Christians. He ordered that John, who was in Ephesus at the time, be sent to Rome where he had him cast into a cauldron of boiling oil. When John miraculously escaped injury, Domitian had him banished to the island of Patmos where it is believed he died of natural causes.

Philip – Preached throughout the areas of Greece, Syria, and Turkey. Tradition holds that Philip converted the wife of the proconsul of the city of Hierapolis through a miraculous healing. This angered the proconsul, and he had Philip, along with his traveling companions, Bartholomew and Mariamne, tortured. Then Philip and Bartholomew were crucified upside down, but Philip continued to preach from his cross. Because of this preaching, Bartholomew was subsequently freed from his cross, but Philip insisted that they not release him and he was martyred.

Bartholomew – While he escaped his first brush with death, alongside Philip, it would eventually catch up with him. History says that he preached the Gospel from Africa to India. While in Armenia, he converted the brother of King Astyages who then had Bartholomew tortured, but the apostle would not renounce his faith. The king then ordered that he be flayed and hung from a cross. When the apostle continued to preach from the cross, tradition says they beheaded him.

Thomas – Often referred to as *Doubting Thomas*, because of his refusal to believe that Jesus had risen from the dead until he could see and feel the wounds received on the cross. Tradition holds that Thomas preached extensively thorough India, where he revered as the patron saint of that country. The king in Calamina ordered him to be tortured and then put into a furnace. When the priests saw that the furnace was having no physical effect on him, they allegedly stabbed him to death.

Matthew – The tax collector, whom Jesus called to follow him, preached in Judea before traveling abroad. Tradition holds that after the death of King Aeglippus, who had been sympathetic to Christians, his successor, Hytacus, killed Matthew by having him nailed to the ground and beheaded.

James the Just – Also referred to as *James the Less*, held the distinction of being the brother of Jesus. It is interesting to note that he has only a marginal role in the Gospels, while Jesus is alive, but after the resurrection he becomes a leading figure and was elected to head the churches of Jerusalem. Some historians say, based upon his listing in some of the Gospels, that James was the older brother of Jesus, possibly a step-brother from a previous marriage of Joseph. This puts James in an altogether unique position. Unlike the other apostles, James *knew* Jesus as something other than a spiritual leader; he knew Him as a brother. As an older brother, I will easily submit that there isn't much that any of my younger siblings could do to convince me they were anywhere near as great as Jesus.

By the lack of inclusion in the early Gospels, we can see that James is not really an *active* participant of his brother's ministry and might not have fully understood things. Yet, after Jesus' death, he becomes one of the leaders of the Christianity movement. He called *James the Just,* because of his great righteousness, and was respected by all seven sects of Judaism. Also noteworthy is James' overall humility. He never seeks to elevate his position, by virtue of his relationship with Jesus, but portrays himself as a humble *servant*.

The Book of Acts gives us the impression that James carried as much authority, or even more, as the other apostles. It is evident that both Peter and Paul hold him in high regard.

When Ananus ben Ananus became the high priest of Jerusalem, after Roman procurator Porcius Festus died, he conspired to rid himself of James. Tradition holds that James, who at the time of his death was in his nineties, was invited to speak at the pinnacle of the temple, but he was summarily thrown from it. The fall however did not kill him and when he began to arise he was set upon and beaten to death. This murder enraged many and led the recently appointed Roman governor Lucceius Albinus to depose the high priest after only three months.

Judas Thaddeus – Also known as Jude, to distinguish him from Judas Iscariot. Tradition shows him preaching throughout the Middle East. While in Syria, he was so effective in converting the populace that the local pagan priests began to lose both power and money. As a result, they apprehended Jude and beat him to death.

Simon the Zealot – He preached the Gospel from Africa to Britannia. At some point he arrived in Syria, around the same time as Jude, where they preached together until Jude's death. Later that same year Simon was also martyred.

Matthias – He was originally part of the larger group of seventy disciples of Jesus. He was chosen to be the apostle to replace Judas Iscariot, after the latter's betrayal of Jesus and after Jesus' ascension. Matthias preached from Judea to Georgia. Tradition holds that he was martyred by being tied to a rock, stoned, and then beheaded.

The deaths of the apostles speak to the depths of hardship and suffering they were willing to endure for their Lord & Savior. We must keep in mind that *all* of their deaths would have occurred while they were actively preaching the risen Christ, at a time rife with anti-Christian sentiment and where information could easily be verified. Had there not been sufficient compelling evidence, it is highly unlikely that Christianity would have managed to survive beyond the mid-point of the first century.

Remember, this is a time of great persecution of the early church, not only from the Roman government, but the Jewish authorities as well. Each viewed this fledgling religion as a fundamental threat to their power and wealth. As both entities previously showed, they had no qualms about striking down the leader, so the followers knew the threats they were facing; yet they began to spread the word far and near.

Flavius Valerius Aurelius Constantinus Augustus, also known as *Constantine the Great*, was the first Roman Emperor to stop the persecution of Christians and to legalize Christianity, but this wasn't until the fourth century.

Beyond the twelve apostles, we also know that there were a number of other early Christians who were persecuted and martyred for their faith. In the Gospel of Luke we are told that Jesus appointed seventy emissaries and sent them out in pairs on a specific mission to spread the word.

During my investigation, I also found several other disciples who were noteworthy:

Luke – The attributed author of the *Gospel of Luke* and *Acts of the Apostles*, it is thought that he was both a doctor and a close disciple of Paul. In **Colossians 4:14**, Paul refers to him as "the beloved physician." It also appears that he was imprisoned. Tradition states that while preaching in Greece, he was hung on an olive tree, but others claim he died of natural causes.

Mark – The attributed author of the Gospel of Mark, he is said to have founded the Church of Alexandria, one of the most important *Episcopal Sees* of early Christianity. Tradition says that when Mark returned to Alexandria, the pagans placed a rope around his neck and dragged him through the streets until he was dead.

Timothy – Was a disciple and companion of Paul and was the subject of two of Paul's letters: **1Timothy** and **2 Timothy**. They had installed him as the head of the church at Ephesus and he served there for fifteen years until his death. Tradition says that when he tried to halt a procession, in honor of the goddess Diana, an angry mob beat him, dragged him through the streets, and then stoned him to death.

Paul – While he was not an original apostle, he is consistently referred to as one and is considered to be one of the most important figures of the early church.

Prior to his conversion he was known as Saul of Tarsus. He was a Roman citizen by birth and came from a devout Jewish family of the Tribe of Benjamin. In his writings he identifies himself as "*a Pharisee, the son of a Pharisee.*" While he was still fairly young, they sent him to Jerusalem to receive his education at the school of Gamaliel. This is important to note, because it establishes that Paul would have had a thorough knowledge of the law.

Prior to his conversion, Paul was an early persecutor of Christians. He believed that the teachings of Jesus violated Mosaic Law and was instrumental in going after Christians in Jerusalem. He was present for the trial and approved of the stoning of one of the original disciples, Saint Stephen. **Acts 8:3**, tell us that, following the death of Stephen, *Saul began to destroy the church. Going from house to house, he dragged off both men and women and put them in prison.* (NIV)

At the time of his conversion, Paul was traveling on the road from Jerusalem to Damascus after he had been granted letters to the synagogues there authorizing him to arrest any Christians and bring them back to Jerusalem. Saul doggedly pursued Christianity, whom he viewed as heretics, in an attempt to crush it and he did not trust the matter to the local authorities.

While traveling to Damascus he was struck down and blinded. He heard a disembodied voice call out to him, "*Saul, Saul, why do you persecute me?*" When he asked who it was, the voice replied, "*I am Jesus, whom you are persecuting.*" **Acts 9:4-5** (NIV)

We cannot overstate the significance of what happened on the road. The conversion of Paul sets the stage for the emergence of one of the most prolific and influential Christians in history. His preaching carried significant weight, because of his background as both a Roman citizen and a former Pharisee. Paul would go on to travel extensively, preaching the Gospel to the gentiles, from Jerusalem to Spain, and suffered greatly. In addition to being imprisoned several times, he was flogged, beaten, and stoned. Tradition says that, like the Apostle Peter, Emperor Nero ordered Paul's execution and he was decapitated.

Before going any further I think it is important to address a common argument for dismissing the deaths of the apostles and early disciples. Many contend that we place too much emphasis upon their deaths. They point out that there are many, especially those in the Muslim world, who offer their lives up for Islam. While this is true, it is important that we look at this matter objectively.

While numerous examples of martyrdom do exist, both in antiquity and modern times, we must also recognize that these people are acting upon *faith*. This is significantly different than what the apostles were acting upon, which was *belief.*

Allow me to provide an example to clarify my position:

Scenario A - I'm watching a baseball game on television with a friend. I have *faith* that my team will win, so I accept a friendly wager. I *do not know* that they will win; it is just my extreme devotion to my team that strengthens me to take that *chance.*

Scenario B – I go to the ballpark where I watch the game live. I sit through every inning only to watch as my team loses to a walk-off home run in the bottom of the ninth. I have witnessed their loss with my own eyes. I leave dejected and head over to my friend's house. He is himself an equally devoted fan of the *other* team, but he had to work and didn't get to see the game. While I am there, he says that he recorded it and asks if I want to watch. I agree, but never tell him I was at the ballpark and watched it live. He then asks me if I want to place a friendly wager.

How many of you would willingly accept that bet, knowing for a *fact* that your team *has already lost*?

Now what if I told you the penalty for losing that bet was a cruel and horrific death?

As I neared the end of my investigation I was left with only two possible outcomes: Either the apostles and disciples preached the Gospel because they had *seen* the risen Christ or they knew that it was all a lie and had all entered into a mutual suicide pact.

For me, the conclusion I reached, based upon the compelling evidence, was that the death and resurrection of Christ was: **<u>FOUNDED</u>**.

Now that I established that Jesus lived, died, and rose from the dead, I needed to consider the spiritual ramifications for humanity.

CHAPTER NINE
(Salvation & Eternal Life)

Jesus said to her, "I am the resurrection and the life. The one who believes in me will live, even though they die." **John 11:25** (NIV)

A few years back, just prior to my retirement, I was driving with another officer when the topic of religion came up. At some point I asked if he thought he was going to Heaven when he died. The answer he gave me was a resounding *yes*, but then I asked him, "*Why?*"

The question caught him a bit off-guard and, after thinking about it for a few minutes, he replied, "*Well, I believe in God, I do good deeds and I go to church regularly. I think I'm a good person.*"

If you ask most people, I would bet that you would get a similar answer. While those are admirable traits, it shines a light on a fundamental misunderstanding about Christianity.

Most times they teach us that believing in God and doing good deeds is the path to Heaven. But if we take a step back and consider these two points for a moment, we realize that Satan *believes* in God and even evil people will do *good deeds* for the ones they love.

In my journey of faith, and I again preface that what you are reading are the conclusions I have come to in *my journey*, I have dealt with several questions and issues, one of which is salvation.

The Catholic Church teaches that, after baptism, if a person commits a mortal sin then he or she can *lose* salvation. They define a mortal sin as a *gravely sinful act*, which can lead to damnation if a person does not repent before death. We consider a sin to be mortal when its quality is such that it leads to a separation of that person from God's saving grace. This means that the sin must be: grave, committed with full knowledge of the sinful act, and done deliberately with complete consent.

To *regain* salvation, a person must perform the sacrament of penance. Catholicism defines the sacrament of penance as having three distinct parts. The *first* of these is contrition, meaning a person must be sorry for his or her sin. *Second*, the person must confess their sin to a priest. The *third* is that they must engage in a redemptive act, such as fasting, prayers, tithing, or doing other such acts as the priest might assign.

But when I looked into what would make up this type of *grave sin*, because I think it is something we should probably know so we can do our best to avoid it, I found that this topic seemed rather *vague*.

Now, I am not a theological expert, by any stretch of the imagination, but I get concerned about a topic that might lead to my *eternal damnation*, especially when there seems to be a sliding-scale approach to things.

Catholic teaching says that, "*Imputability and responsibility for an action can be diminished or even nullified by ignorance, inadvertence, duress, fear, habit, inordinate attachments, and other psychological or social factors.*" (**Catechism of the Catholic Church. Second Edition. Part Three, Section One, Chapter One, #1735**)

Habit? Seriously?

So if I just have a habit of doing horrible things, the gravity of my sin can be *diminished*?

As I mentioned before, I grew up in the Catholic Church. I went through baptism, confirmation, communion, penance (confession), and I was an altar boy. I attended confession regularly, but I will admit that I never *fully* confessed my sins. Let's be honest, what twelve-year-old boy will admit to *everything*? Since the church tells us that the sacraments are necessary for salvation, I naturally had several questions.

My career in law enforcement has often caused me to be creative on a lot of issues. Some call it playing *Devil's Advocate*, others have more colorful names for it, but I like to think of it as looking at all the angles. As I considered the Church's teaching I wondered about the following scenario:

An adolescent girl of seventeen, who was raised in the Catholic Church, and received all of the sacraments for her age, has pre-marital sex and gets pregnant. Her parents are divorced and she lives with her mother, who is now an avowed atheist and feminist activist. Since she is a minor, she falls under her mother's authority, who demands that she get an abortion. She has no one to turn to, so she complies with her wishes and aborts the baby. Under Code of Canon Law, they treat abortion as a crime and her actions would cause an *ipso facto, latae sententiae* (Latin for "by the fact itself, sentence passed") excommunication.

However, while she is of legal age according to the church (over 16), can she be held responsible if she acted under *duress* and how do we define that duress? Is she in fact *honoring* her mother by submitting to her will, typically treated as an excellent thing, or is this an example where she wouldn't be committing a sin if she didn't honor her? What happens if she is okay with it at the time of the abortion, but then has an epiphany later in life and realizes just what she has done? If she cries out to God for forgiveness, will he reject her?

Now I admit that this is *extreme* thinking, but I am of the belief that if we can think it, it can happen. Call me crazy, but if I have these types of questions in *my* head, then we might want to take a step back and re-evaluate things.

For a moment, I want you to consider what I said about crime back in Chapter Six. We as human beings are always looking for an excuse; something that will differentiate our bad behavior from the next person. What distinction do we make for a soldier who kills to protect his country? Most contend that a soldier is simply following orders so there wouldn't be any ramifications. What then shall we say about the *Waffen SS* soldier? Over the years I have spoken to several of these combat veterans who said they were just following orders as well. Do earthly rulers get to decide which acts are justified and which are not? Where is the line drawn between freedom fighter and terrorist?

Consider that The Founding Fathers waged a war of rebellion against the rightful government of King George III and killed his duly appointed representatives. Had the rebellion been quashed, they would have rightfully faced death for their actions. The militiamen who fought for this country were following orders.

Over the years I have had many discussions about sin and I recognize that it is a very sensitive subject. The push-back I get, when I ask someone what makes their sin less than mine, usually tells me I am hitting a nerve.

When we take a hard look at, we conclude that we are trying to make *excuses* for our behavior to another human being, but we seem to forget that it is not another human being who we are being judged by.

In the past I have submitted the following question:

A woman goes to the supermarket and does the food shopping for her family. After the cashier gets done checking out her order, she hands the woman back her change. As she walks away, the woman notices that the cashier has given her an extra twenty-dollar bill in her change. It is a period of difficult financial times for her family, so the woman pockets the extra money and walks out of the store without saying anything.

Then I pose a second scenario:

A man is checking out at the grocery store. As the cashier is ringing up his order, he asks her for a pack of cigarettes. As the woman turns her back toward him, to get the requested item, the man reaches over and removes a twenty-dollar bill from the open register and slips it into his pocket.

Who has committed the worst sin?

By far the most common answer I get is the man, but is it really correct?

It would be very easy to agree with the assessment that the man has committed the worst sin, as he has actively stolen money, but we only reach that conclusion when we inject our own bias into the equation. We want to believe that the man is more at fault, but when we impartially look at each act, through the eyes of a perfect God, both are sins.

As I said before, human beings try to qualify things to make ourselves feel better, but do we understand the potential *spiritual damage* we are doing?

Most of the problems I see, coming out of Christianity, do not originate with God, but with man's interpretation. I once had a chat with someone who described themselves as being anti-religion. I asked them what specifically they took issue with, regarding Jesus' teachings? After a while it became obvious they weren't so much anti-religious as they were *anti-religious dogma*.

Repeatedly, I have seen people walk away from the church, not because of the message, but because of the messenger. It's not a *God* problem, it's a *people* problem. We can't just be happy delivering God's message of salvation; we have to interject ourselves into it.

Jesus said, *"I am the way and the truth and the life. No one comes to the Father except through me."* **John 14:6** (NIV)

He didn't say, "I am the way and the truth and the life. No one comes to the Father except through me, *Bob, Mary, Tony, and Jimmy."*

So when we see people walking away from the church, and abandoning their relationship with God, we have to ask ourselves, *why?*

Few will like the answer.

The condition of the church at large is, in many ways, similar to that of the Jewish temple in Jesus' time. Not that the church doesn't do exemplary work, but it doesn't take an advanced investigative mind to see it is rife with systemic corruption and abuse. Nothing like being chastised for *your* sins by folks engaged in illicit sex acts with minors and money laundering.

One of the biggest complaints that I hear is from folks who complain about the staggering amount of wealth that has been amassed by religious organizations, while children around the world continue to starve to death.

Over the years I worked in some impoverished neighborhoods. I'm not talking, '*my parents promised me steak and potatoes, but all I got was a PB&J sandwich and milk,*' poor. No, I'm talking: *I haven't eaten in days*, poor.

It never ceased to amaze me when I sat in my radio car and watched the *Bishop* pull up to his church driving a brand new Cadillac and wearing a bespoke suit. It seemed surreal to see this contrast between wealth and poverty play out before my eyes. If it troubled me, I had to wonder what God thought about it. Yet it is not a scene that is only played out among poor communities. Turn on the TV any Sunday and you can see a parade of the same charlatans. They hide behind the word of God, all the while doing more to line their own pockets. They are modern day Sadducees, wolves in clerics clothing, who thump their Bibles to the crowd, telling them they need to give *more* in order to spread God's word, then jump in their chauffeured, luxury vehicles and head to the airport to board their private jets.

Yes, it is true that they represent only a small fraction of today's clergy, where the average salary is only about $45,000, but they are its most prominent face. What kind of message do you think it sends to someone living meal to meal, when they hear that some pastor has an estimated self-worth of nearly one billion dollars? Or that the Vatican, not the Catholic Church, has a worth estimated to be between $10-$15 billion dollars.

And what about the so-called *prosperity preachers?* Those who change the Bible to teach their own version of the Gospel? Well, if their bank accounts are any indication, then business is booming. So is it any wonder why people get angry with God, when they see His earthly representatives living like rock stars?

The problem is that these folks aren't working for God, they are working for themselves, and they are using the Bible for their personal self-enrichment, just like in the days of Jesus, but once again God gets the bad rap.

When you tear away the façade, the problem is, and always will be, human. All we have to do is look back to the Garden of Eden to see that we do not make excellent choices; even when we are living in paradise.

It reminds me of the old argument regarding communism. Despite the overwhelming evidence that it doesn't work, proponents continue to suggest that *real communism* hasn't been tried.

Perhaps, in some small way, they have a point. If I was to get together with a half dozen other families and start our own community, we might have a successful communist commune. We could each share in the division of work and the fruits of our labor, but once you get beyond that small nucleus is where the waters get muddied. Communism fails when people stop thinking about each other and find a way to elevate themselves. As groups become bigger, they require an administrative group who oversee things. Once you begin to live off of someone else's hard work, the system declines and then you need someone to *enforce* things for you, to keep the workers productive.

I imagine this was what Jesus meant when He advised the rich man to give his wealth to the poor and *then* follow Him. Unfortunately, the church has now become that rich man. One look at the Vatican's art collection tells you all you need to know.

I would like to say this is a recent phenomenon, but it is not. Jesus even warned us when he said, *"Keep watch over yourselves and all the flock of which the Holy Spirit has made you overseers. Be shepherds of the church of God, which he bought with his own blood. I know that after I leave, savage wolves will come in among you and will not spare the flock. Even from your own number men will arise and distort the truth in order to draw away disciples after them. So be on your guard! Remember that for three years I never stopped warning each of you night and day with tears."* **Acts 20:28-31** (NIV)

Now, let me state for the record that I am not *anti-wealth*. I know that in my life I have been blessed, but I have also known both good times and hard. I don't think God wants us to live in abject poverty, but neither do I believe that He wants us to live in multi-million dollar mansions, while a few miles down the road some child will go to sleep hungry for the fourth night in a row! More importantly, *we* should not want this.

So with God and our salvation, where should we look for answers?

Well, the Bible is probably the place to start.

Ephesians 2: 8-9, *"For it is by grace you have been saved, through faith, and this is not from yourselves, it is the gift of God."* (NIV)

I remember as a young man being told that, *"If something sounds too good to be true, then it probably is."*

Under normal circumstances I think this is very sound advice, but there is an exception to every rule and this is one of those times. A lot of uncertainty about our fate stems from the fact that we are told things by preachers, instead of learning things on our own. As a result, we do not fully comprehend God and this is understandable; after all, He is God.

From the beginning of time we have used our *free will* in the worst possible ways. In the Old Testament we are told that, *"Love the LORD your God with all your heart and with all your soul and with all your strength."* **Deuteronomy 6:5** (NIV)

Yet we continually choose other things first and, by doing so, we sin and dishonor God.

Consider for a moment the gravity of that statement. We are not dishonoring a peer, a parent, a boss, a hero, a president, or a pope. We are dishonoring the Great I Am, the Creator, the Lord God Almighty.

Romans 6:23, tells us that, *"the wages of sin is death."* How then can we expect that a just and perfect God would act unjustly and not punish us? The answer is that we cannot. We were all condemned to death until Jesus.

"The next day he saw Jesus coming toward him, and said, 'Behold, the Lamb of God, who takes away the sin of the world!'" **John 1:29** (NIV)

The only solution to the problem of humanity's sinful nature was that someone needed to make atonement, but whom?

Many of us would be willing to lay down our lives for a loved one. Some of us might even lay down our lives for a close friend. A remarkably smaller group would lay down their lives for a stranger, but who among us would lay down their lives for someone who despised them? Who among us would allow themselves to be insulted, spit on, horrifically beaten, and still surrender their life for their attackers?

And now you can begin to understand why humanity needed a savior.

"For God so loved the world that he gave his one and only Son, that whoever believes in him shall not perish but have eternal life." **John 3:16** (NIV)

There is a song by one of my favorite Christian groups, **Casting Crowns**, called, *"Who am I?"* written by **John Mark Hall**. The lyrics are very powerful and include the lines:

"Who am I, that the Lord of all the earth,

Would care to know my name,

Would care to feel my hurt?"

Yet we seem to forget that God is not some impersonal deity. The first line of the Lord's Prayer is: "*Our Father, who art in heaven, hallowed be thy name.*"

Our **Father**. Let that sink in.

He is not just the Creator, but we are told by Jesus that He is *our* Father, and that is precisely the way we should see Him.

The first time I watched the *Passion of the Christ,* I openly wept. There is a scene where Jesus is carrying his cross, as he heads to Golgotha. At one point, He falls in the street under the heavy weight and Mary rushes toward Him. It cuts to a flashback that shows Mary comforting her adolescent son after He falls while running. It is a very visceral scene, because in that moment it shows the humanity of both Jesus and Mary. That bond between parent and child. After the flashback, we see Mary attempting to comfort the beaten and bloodied Jesus who says, "See mother, I make all things new."

I admit it was like a physical *gut-punch* for me. To this day I cannot watch that scene without feeling devastated. As parents, we have all raced to the sound of our child's cries. Want to see uncontrollable rage? Put yourself between a parent and their hurting child. Yet I watch that, along with reading the Bible, and understand that Jesus made the choice to endure all of these things for me, a sinner. He was the only one willing to lay down His life, to save those who despised Him, while we were *still in sin*. Yet some would tell us that this isn't enough. That we must somehow add to this by works and deeds.

I ask you to watch this movie, to allow yourself to see just what constituted a Roman scourging and crucifixion, and ask yourself if there is anything that you can *add* to that sacrifice?

Jesus had the skin flayed from His back? No problem, I shoveled Mrs. Smith's walkway.

Jesus got nailed to a cross? Well, I worked thirty minutes overtime last week and *didn't* put in for it.

To quote Ralph Wiggum, from The Simpson's: "*I'm helping!*"

The reality is that either Christ took upon Himself the punishment for our sins or He didn't. He was either the *Lamb of God*, the perfect sacrifice, or He wasn't.

Once again we are interjecting ourselves into this formula through our own hubris. Some of us want to believe that we can add to our salvation; that, by some *act of goodness* we are working in unison with Jesus, and thereby merit some of the credit.

We are like the bat-boy on the championship baseball team who gets a World Series ring by picking up discarded bats. Yeah, *technically* you were a member of the team, but….

Christ died for our sins, paying the ultimate price to get us right with God, and the only thing we need to do is accept that gift.

Consider what the Apostle Paul tells us in his first letter to Timothy, "*This is a faithful saying, and worthy of all acceptation, that Christ Jesus came into the world to save sinners; of whom I am chief. Howbeit for this cause I obtained mercy, that in me first Jesus Christ might shew forth all longsuffering, for a pattern to them which should hereafter believe on him to life everlasting. Now unto the King eternal, immortal, invisible, the only wise God, be honour and glory for ever and ever. Amen.*" **1 Timothy 1: 15-17** (KJV)

Paul pulls no punches. He says definitively that Christ came into the world to save sinners. Jesus had already been resurrected by the time Paul writes this letter and he admits that he is still a sinner.

It is such an important theme that he follows this up in **Romans**, where he says, "*So I find this law at work: Although I want to do good, evil is right there with me. For in my inner being I delight in God's law; but I see another law at work in me, waging war against the law of my mind and making me a prisoner of the law of sin at work within me. What a wretched man I am! Who will rescue me from this body that is subject to* *death? Thanks be to God, who delivers me through Jesus Christ our Lord!"* **Romans 7:21-25** (NIV)

Not for one moment would I ever claim to be as strong a Christian as the Apostle Paul. So if he believed that he remained a sinner, doing the very things he hated, and needed Jesus to save him, than who am I to believe I hold a different place?

The answer is that salvation is through Jesus alone.

Jesus died to save the world and the only thing we are required to do is *accept* it.

Yet, people continue to struggle with this, and I think it reveals a fundamental problem that we seem to have. Grace shows us the true extent of our *lack of autonomy*.

We, as a society, celebrate our independence. We marvel at the accomplishments we have achieved, from harnessing the awesome power of fire to putting a man on the moon. Yet, with the most significant thing in our life, our spiritual salvation, we are utterly powerless and completely dependent on God. For some, who view themselves as *masters of their own destiny*, this is a very unappealing premise and they have told me they flatly reject this premise. It seems as if they truly believe that their altruistic acts are all that is required to achieve salvation.

Some of us have become so focused on constructing a spiritual resume of *good deeds*, that we are rejecting eternity because we cannot accept the gift.

Accepting Jesus' death as payment for my sins isn't a cop-out; it is often a very hard thing to do. The moment you realize what He had to suffer through, to pay for your sins, brings home the significance of every single sin in your life. Each lie, each theft, each unkind word, is like another lash He had to endure. You face the awesome reality of just how unworthy you were and just how much He loves you.

There are many people who mock God. They consider themselves intellectually superior than those who believe a fairy tale. My question to them is this: *"If I believe in a fairy tale, that Jesus died for my sins, and that belief then causes me to live my life, not perfectly, but in trying to be a good person to others, what harm have I done? What have I lost?"*

Have I wasted anything by accepting Christ's death and resurrection as payment for my sins?

What cost is there in surrendering myself to this?

If I am wrong, what have I lost? I led a moral life, was kind to others, and then I died.

But, and this is an *enormous but*, if I am right and you are wrong, and there is an eternal life, will you find yourself wishing you had believed in the *fairy tale*?

I don't know about you, but I am not willing to take that chance.

So mock me if you must, but I will proclaim loudly that Jesus Christ is my Lord and Savior.

CHAPTER TEN
(Where Was God?)

"Where was God on the morning of September 11th, 2001?"

My journey has resulted in my understanding that this really isn't the question that we need to ask.

No, once again, the real question is, *"Ayeka?"*

"Where are you?"

Our actions today do not differ from those of Adam and Eve. It is not God who has walked away from us, but we who have lost our walk with God.

Two thousand years ago Jesus gave us two simple commandments: *Love God and love one another.* Yet two thousand years later we still cannot find it within us to live by those two basic tenets.

Whether in modern times or those of antiquity, man cannot cease being inhumane to our brothers and sisters. We have slaughtered each other by the hundreds of millions during wars. We have starved each other, enslaved one another, and committed acts of barbaric torture.

Some will claim that we did many of these atrocities *in the name of God* and I will not dispute that, but I will say that we must never blame God for the darkness which is in our own hearts. Free will means that we alone are responsible for our own actions.

When a madman goes on a killing spree on behalf of the demonic voices in his head, we marginalize them and call them *insane.* Yet when someone claims that God told him to commit some loathsome act we refer to them as a *religious zealot;* proving once again that Satan gets a pass, while God gets all the blame.

When we as parents take the time to warn our children not to do something, but they choose to do it when we are not looking, the fault rests with them, not us. That does not mean that we don't hurt for them, but we must recognize that this was a lesson they had to learn on their own. As humans, we continue to struggle with this century after century. Just like a petulant child who refuses to accept any responsibility for their actions, we look to blame our divine parent because we did something wrong.

How could God allow this?

Why did God make this?

Where was God?

This continual blame game always looks to point the finger as far away from us as possible, so we can avoid any of the responsibility for the actions *we* took.

Yes, sometimes in our life when we go through periods of extreme difficulty; life altering circumstances involving hurt, tragedy and even death. Where dreadful things happen to wonderful people and we just cannot make sense of it all. It is during times like this, when we are in the middle of the fire, that we often struggle to make sense of our predicament.

One day I was watching a show on television that featured a man who created custom knives from scrap metal. He would find a discarded piece that had outlived its former life and create a new use for it. One time it was a leaf-spring from an old car and another time it was a wrench.

I watched him repeatedly heat the blade up in his forge and then hammer it into shape. A process he would repeat over and over until he formed the metal into the desired shape. He would take someone else's trash and turn it into something beautiful. It left me with the impression that he was clearly a master knife maker. However, in a moment of clarity, I soon realized that this process was only apparent to those of us watching from the *outside*. From the perspective of the steel, things most likely would have seemed a whole lot *different*.

It's the same thing with humans. Often, when you are in the middle of adversity, it's hard to tell if you're being hammered into shape and refined, or just being pummeled and burned until you reach the end.

Several years ago I got a phone call from my old Lieutenant, Paul Murphy, who shared with me that he had been diagnosed with cancer attributed to 9/11. In a way it shocked me, but at the same time it didn't. I'd heard stories about the medical studies being conducted on first responders and the findings that pointed to the exponentially higher number of cancer rates between the WTC community and the general public. It became the *dirty little secret* that the government had lied to all of us when they said the air was *safe*.

Hearing him say that he had cancer made me feel guilty. He had a wife and two young daughters. It seemed so incredibly unfair. Here was a man who was a hero on 9/11, who had put himself in harm's way to save others and was now paying for it with his very life.

Over the years we would talk on the phone and chat on social media. No matter what tests he was going through, the chemo treatments or the different surgeries, he always had an upbeat attitude. Once he got done with the latest round of medical issues, he would proclaim that he was going back to the gym and getting 'huge'….. If you knew Paul, you knew there was no way he would ever be mistaken for *huge*. He also loved pizza, so every Friday was pizza night and he would share with us the latest choice. Simply put, despite being dealt a really shitty hand, Paul had the best damn attitude that anyone could possibly have.

And then one cold January day I got the fateful message from his daughter that he had passed away.

To say I was dumbfounded would be a gross understatement. We had talked only a few days earlier and he said that he was feeling better, yet now he was gone. I felt numb inside and, for a very brief moment, it took my mind off my own 9/11 cancer diagnosis which I had received just a few weeks prior.

In my introduction, I alluded to the fact that the reason this book had taken so long to write was because I was waiting on the right words from God. Those words finally took form in my life, just before Christmas, when I took the call that confirmed the biopsy they had taken tested positive for cancer.

It is truly a moment that no one can prepare you for and yet there it was, like the 800lb gorilla in the room, staring me in the face, or at the very least ringing in my ear.

In facing your own mortality it is very easy to become bitter; to blame God. Over the years I talked with a lot of folks who shared with me the *one-sided* screaming matches they've had with Him. How they hated Him for what He *allowed* to happen. Now here I was getting the diagnosis that most people are terrified to get and yet I felt no animus toward God.

For a moment I wondered if it was just shock; that the full weight of it had just not hit me. But as the days turned into weeks and then into months, I realized there was no resentment, no bitterness toward God. A part of me feels that this happened so I could write this story. As I said in the beginning, it's hard to accept advice from someone who doesn't have any skin in the game.

Don't get me wrong, I am angry, but that anger rests squarely on the shoulders of those responsible: the terrorists, who committed those heinous acts, and their state sponsors.

It wasn't God that *committed* those acts, I don't care how you twist, contort, massage, or boldly proclaim it, and it wasn't God that *inspired* them.

"Well, if you're God is so loving then explain the horrible things He does in the Old Testament!"

Have you heard this one before? I know I have and I would be remiss if I didn't take a moment to address it. It has become the battle-cry of atheists in denouncing religion and I sometimes have to fight the urge to reply, *"How can you claim that God does horrible things when in the same breath you deny that the Bible is even real?"*

At first glance, the God of the Old Testament seems to be completely different from the one in the New Testament, and many Christians have a problem when they are confronted with this accusation, but is He really different?

I opened Chapter Five with the statement that almost everyone who sits down to read the Bible usually jumps right in at **Genesis 1**. But, as the *wherefores* and *begets* start to pile up, their interest soon wanes and they get that glassy-eyed look. Maybe they even make it as far as **Leviticus**, but for most readers, by the time they get to **Numbers** it is game over. So they have no foundation when the attack comes from non-believers. They have not read **Joshua** or **Judges**.

If you read some of the passages, the tales look like they could be ripped from the pages of a horror book. According to the accusations, just about every page of the Old Testament is filled with entire cities burned to the ground and entire populations being annihilated. It portrays God as a wrathful deity who is constantly directing His people to commit atrocities. Even worse, by today's standards, we are told that God destroys the cities of Sodom and Gomorrah, because they had given in to sexual immortality.

It leaves many Christians hemming and hawing, as God's accusers just smirk. This is the place where the proverbial rubber meets the road.

The truth is that God is God.

We can sugar coat things, we can *explain away* things, or we can repeat what He tells us when He gives Moses the Ten Commandments: *"for I, the LORD your God, am a jealous God, punishing the children for the sin of the parents to the third and fourth generation of those who hate me, but showing love to a thousand generations of those who love me and keep my commandments."* **Exodus 20: 5-6** (NIV)

Some Christians don't want to address the darker aspects of the Bible, but that is entirely disingenuous and it is also dangerous. Unfortunately, just as we do with Satan, we seem to have this desire to *rebrand* God into what we want Him to be and not who He is. We have created this illusion that God is like a divine Santa Claus; an affable, perhaps slightly quirky, peaceful little fellow who wants nothing more than to lavish us with outstanding gifts. We forget that we are God's *creation* and, more importantly, we forget the *awesome power* of God.

The average Bible comprises nearly a million words and comes in at around twelve hundred pages. It is easy to pick and choose things to attack, but when you look at it in its entirety; you see things as they are intended.

In our post Garden of Eden existence, man had slowly, but surely, turned the Earth into a cold and cruel place. We had given into our basest desires; all while murdering and enslaving those who stood in our way.

The Bible is the story of God, but it also the story of us and highlights exactly why God has taken the action He has. When we look to attack God, for all the unpleasant things, we again fail to look at who is at fault in all of this. Had we obeyed the rules, in the Garden of Eden, the story would have ended with **Genesis 1: 31**, but it didn't because *we* couldn't follow the rules.

It reminds me of the joke where a member of the government confronts an old Indian chief. The man says, *"Chief Red Bear, you have observed the white man for ninety years. You've seen all the things he has done, the wars and the progress in technological advancements. After considering all these events, in your opinion, where did the white man go wrong?"*

The Chief thought for a moment and then replied, *"When white man comes to our land, there were no taxes and no debt. There was plenty of buffalo, deer, and beaver. The water was clean, the medicine man was free, and the women did all the work. The Indian man spent all day hunting and fishing, and all night making love."*

Then the Chief leaned back and smiled knowingly. *"Only the white man dumb enough to think he could improve a system like that."*

Yet from the beginning we have tried to change things, not to God's way, but to ours. One of the primary reasons we have such a hard time reconciling the Old and the New Testament's is because we have not taken the time to understand the passages or God.

Humanity is in the shape it is in, not because of God, but because of our unwillingness to obey Him from the beginning. The horror and calamity detailed in the Old Testament directly results from humanities callous nature, not because of God being arbitrary and capricious.

We have lost sight of the fact that God is the ultimate judge and we must respect Him or pay the price.

I will stop at this point because, while I felt that I needed to address it, it is such a serious topic that I cannot do it justice within the framework of this book. But I would encourage you to read through both the Old and New Testaments. There are many online resources and books that will help guide you through them so you can understand them better. Study them within the context of the *day and age that they were written*, not through the rose colored, politically correct lenses that man has fashioned for this era.

As I said, we as human beings only see the snap-shot of our life, but God sees the entire movie. He is, after all, the Great I Am; the Alpha and the Omega.

We are living in the world He created. As the Creator, He knows everything about us. Despite our propensity for doing bad, He can, and does, still use it for His good. If we are searching for answers, then we need to go back to the very beginning and I cannot think of a better story to illustrate this than that of Joseph.

The story begins in **Genesis 37** and it is such an important story that it takes up more than a fifth of the entire book. In it we are told the story of how Joseph is betrayed by his jealous brothers and sold into slavery. He is taken from his homeland and transported to Egypt, where he ends up working for Potiphar, the captain of Pharaoh's guard. Eventually he ends up becoming Potiphar's personal servant, but it is a double-edged sword. After rebuffing advances by the captain's wife, he ends up in prison after she makes false allegations of rape against him.

I can see how being betrayed by your family, who originally wanted to kill you, would make some people ask, "Where was God?" Not to mention being sold into slavery, then being falsely accused of a crime you didn't commit and languishing in an Egyptian prison for years.

We are taught to believe in justice and when we see injustice we struggle to make sense of it. Well, in the case of Joseph we are given the answer to our question and it would serve us well to apply it to our present dilemma as well.

Joseph had been given a special ability by God. He had the ability to interpret dreams. When Pharaoh was faced with a dream that no one could answer, Joseph suddenly found himself before the ruler of Egypt. Joseph explained that the dreams were a harbinger of things to come. He warned Pharaoh that Egypt would face seven years of abundance which would then be followed by seven years of famine, and he advised him to store up grains. As a result, Egypt survived the ensuing famine. Joseph eventually rose up and attained the position of *vizier*, the second highest authority in all of Egypt.

To put it in layman's terms, Joseph was a modern day prime minister who ran all of Egypt for Pharaoh. A significant achievement for anyone, let alone a Jew who'd been betrayed by his siblings, sold into slavery, and jailed in a foreign land.

In **Genesis 50: 19-20,** we are told that when Joseph met with his brothers' years later, they rightly feared he would have them executed for their crimes against him. *"But Joseph said to them, 'Don't be afraid. Am I in the place of God? You intended to harm me, but God intended it for good to accomplish what is now being done, the saving of many lives.'"* (NIV)

Despite the evil machinations that man had begun, God had other ideas. It was true then and it is true now.

This doesn't negate the tragedy of what occurred that fateful morning of September 11th, nor does it minimize the tragedies that occur daily, but we must take comfort that, even if we do not understand why, God is in control of all things, at all times.

As I have said, I have gone through difficult periods in my life and I have always found comfort and strength in Paul's words, *"And we know that in all things God works for the good of those who love him, who have been called according to his purpose. For those God foreknew he also predestined to be conformed to the image of his Son, that he might be the firstborn among many brothers and sisters. And those he predestined, he also called; those he called, he also justified; those he justified, he also glorified. What, then, shall we say in response to these things? If God is for us, who can be against us?"* **Romans 8: 28-31** (NIV)

I believe that we question things when we are afraid. We see the evil and brutality of the world and recognize that we are the cause, not the solution. Our hearts and minds *hope* for an answer, but we must understand that hope will not provide it, just like hoping for the answers won't help a child taking a test. We must take the time to educate ourselves about God; about His laws and about His promise.

"In this world you will have trouble. But take heart! I have overcome the world." **John 16:33** (NIV)

Christians understand that God does not promise us an easy life, but we are promised an eternal one.

In the end, we should spend more time working on our personal relationship with God, instead of asking where He is during times of difficulty. There will always be hardships in life, but instead of blaming Him or asking Him to fix it, perhaps we should focus more on our behavior that has caused it. Maybe then we would have less tragic events to deal with in the future.

There were five Nelson's killed on September 11th, 2001. I firmly believe I would have been the sixth, if it wasn't for a pack of cigarettes, but what made me choose to quit quitting? As I said before, I earnestly believe that it was a matter of divine intervention; that it wasn't my time, and that I was spared because God was going to use me for His purpose.

So for those who have asked: *"Where was God on September 11th, 2001?"* The conclusion I have reached is that he was right where He has always been.

It's understandable that we only focus on the *photographs* of our life, because I do not believe that we could handle the full scope and depth of the *movie.* There will be events that occur, that defy explanation, that cause us to drop to our knees in anger or prayer or both, but we must learn to realize that not everything that occurs is for *us.*

We can use the free will that we possess for either our benefit or demise. When the terrorists attacked that day they were acting on the latter. But despite the tragedy, and enormous loss of life, I still believe God was there, working in unseen ways. That you are here, reading this book, speaks to that.

Was I saved that day for a reason? I believe so.

Was I given this illness, *after* I became an author, so I would know how to share this message? Again, I think I was.

Do I wish that I didn't have this? Of course I do!

But, as a Christian, I am reminded of what Jesus said in the Garden of Gethsemane: *"My Father, if it is possible, may this cup be taken from me. Yet not as I will, but as you will."* **Matthew 26:39** (NIV)

In the end, God is where he always is, in *our hearts,* but what we do with that relationship will ultimately remain our choice.

CHAPTER ELEVEN

(Pandemics – Tragedy Beyond 9/11)

As I sit here doing the re-edit for this book, I cannot help but acknowledge that it is happening at the holy days of Passover and Easter, as the world is being consumed by the Chinese Corona Virus pandemic. I felt that I would be remiss if I didn't use this opportunity to address what is going on.

I recently saw a meme on the internet that said, *"Commemorating not getting killed by a plague, during a plague that you hope you're not getting killed by, is probably as Jewish as you can get."*

A moment of levity in a bleak time, but it also struck me as being poignant. Our history is littered with examples of humanity going through periods of tragedy. From wars that claimed the lives of millions of people, to plagues that claimed tens of millions more.

Now we suffer through yet another world-wide pandemic known as the Chinese Corona Virus (COVID-19). I know that for my NYPD family, this has been especially difficult. At the time I am writing this, we have lost thirty active members and that number will surely increase. This does not count the retired members, many of them 9/11 survivors, who have also died from the virus.

It is hard to imagine how God could allow a tragedy such as this to spread across the globe, but again we must take a step back if we are to understand what we are dealing with.

At the beginning of this pandemic, the Chinese government took extreme measures to promote this virus as being naturally occurring. They claimed that it had originated in a *wet market* in Wuhan Province, a sentiment echoed by the World Health Organization. But, as the weeks turned into months, evidence emerged that it likely escaped from the Wuhan Institute of Virology; China's first level 4 biosafety facility. At present, there are over fifty of these BSL-4 facilities worldwide. While most of these facilities are benign, and serve a greater scientific purpose as we try to understand and fight disease, there is no doubt that we can also use them for nefarious intent.

While the Chinese government *technically* recognizes five religions: Buddhism, Taoism, Catholicism, Protestantism, and Islam, the government officially espouses state atheism and prohibits party members from practicing religion while in office.

It should be noted that, in Xi Jinping's China, they have cracked down on organized religion, which is seen as a threat to the state's power. Muslim's have been interned in camps, Buddhists have been forced to pledge allegiance to the ruling Communist Party, and they have forced Christian churches to take down crosses. So while there is religion in China, the faithful can only practice it freely if the state sanctions it. It is part of a process called *Sinicization* in which they fuse religion with Chinese socialist thought.

Why do I mention this?

Well, when you place the state at the highest pinnacle, then there is nothing you cannot do for the benefit of the state. Now, I am not saying that things are any better in the west. History provides us with a treasure trove of religious hypocrisy; acts of barbarity committed in the name of God.

Which is worse? That is ultimately left up for you to decide.

But as we examine this age in which we live, we cannot help but once again question whether we are blaming God for what are essentially man-made problems.

I saw a post on social media the other day from a friend asking for prayers. She related that the daughter of one of her friends had been involved in a serious automobile accident and was in ICU. While the overwhelming majority of replies were positive, one struck me as particularly disturbing. In response to a prayer request, the reply was, *"If faith and prayer is all you have, you certainly don't have much."*

Beyond the obvious lack of empathy to what this family is going through, it serves as a stark reminder of the actual problem we face. Man's inhumanity to man.

I am reminded of **2 Chronicles 7:14** *"If my people, who are called by my name, will humble themselves and pray and seek my face and turn from their wicked ways, then I will hear from heaven, and I will forgive their sin and will heal their land."* (NIV)

What many people cannot comprehend in this passage is the statement: If **my** people. The sad fact is that not everyone that walks the face of the Earth is called to be a child of God. A cursory examination of history shows that many revel in the fact that they don't believe, some going so far as to proudly proclaiming that they are atheists.

Galatians 6:7-8 makes it crystal clear, *"Do not be deceived: God cannot be mocked. A man reaps what he sows. Whoever sows to please their flesh, from the flesh will reap destruction; whoever sows to please the Spirit, from the Spirit will reap eternal life."* (NIV)

Neither the joys of this world nor the pain are lasting. But if we take a hard look at the troubles we face, is it really fair to blame God? Did God unleash this pandemic on the world? No, man accomplished this and it is an issue I will explore in the next chapter.

History provides us with example after example of man's cruelty to each other. War, poverty, slavery, & tyrannical governments have existed for millennia.

1 Peter 5:8 says, *"Be sober, be vigilant, because your adversary the devil walketh about as a roaring lion, seeking whom he may devour."* (NIV)

We are warned that we should be alert, but many do not understand the dangers. Some fear *possession* by demons, but remember, Satan is a deceiver. He doesn't have to take physical possession of you to achieve success. He can accomplish monumental things with just a willing mind and an apathetic heart.

We are told that we are a global *community* of nearly eight billion people, but war, poverty, slavery, & tyrannical governments persist.

Is it God who is at fault when a wealthy government class turns a blind eye to the needs of their population? No.

Is it God who is at fault when a government creates a bioweapon that is suddenly unleashed on the world? No.

Is Satan at work? Yes.

"The god of this age has blinded the minds of unbelievers, so that they cannot see the light of the gospel that displays the glory of Christ, who is the image of God." **2 Corinthians 4:4** (NIV)

We live in a world unlike any other in the history of man. To say that our children have access to a treasure trove of information, in the palm of their hands, isn't hollow. Estimates are that the four major players, Google, Amazon, Microsoft, and Facebook, store at least 1,200 petabytes of information between them. To give you an idea of what that entails, one petabyte of average MP3-encoded songs would take 2000 years to play. Sadly, this knowledge is often wasted and abused.

In the nearly two millennia since Christ walked the earth, we have done very little to achieve his challenge to love God and love one another. Instead, we submit to our base desires; choosing to acquiesce to Satan's whispered encouragement of choosing self, over God's admonitions to love one another.

The Corona Virus is the perfect storm that never should have happened, but it highlights everything wrong with humanity. Some people will contend that this research is important, and I will not argue that point, however it is not the research that I find fault with, but the response. Rather than admit that there was a failure, the response from China's government appears to have been one lie after another, as they tried to protect their *image*. How many people died because of this vanity? Well, certainly more than ever needed to.

As of this date, the official number of cases in China stands at just under eighty-four thousand and a mortality rate of forty-six hundred. No one, except the World Health Organization, believes this is an accurate accounting. Contrast this with the United States, where the number of cases and mortality is ten times that of China. It begs the question, why are they lying?

In China, and in so many other places around the world, the government must always be right. If we see the government as being unable to protect themselves and their citizens, then their power is at risk. Lies become necessary to shift blame away from failed policies.

Governments are not detached entities; they are composed of living, breathing people. These people are not infallible and given the opportunity most will take steps to preserve their own self-interest before anyone else. I am sure that you, like I, have heard the cautionary tales of honorable people that ran for office only to change once they got elected. But instead of holding these people to a higher standard, we idly sit on the sidelines while they enrich themselves.

Most have heard the quote from Sir John Dalberg-Acton, the 19th century British politician, that says, *"Power tends to corrupt and absolute power corrupts absolutely,"* but that is only a snippet. That sentence is actually from a letter Lord Acton wrote to Bishop Mandell Creighton, Church of England. It is part of a series of letters concerning the moral problem of writing history about the Inquisition.

"I cannot accept your canon that we are to judge Pope and King unlike other men, with a favourable presumption that they did no wrong. If there is any presumption it is the other way against holders of power, increasing as the power increases. Historic responsibility has to make up for the want of legal responsibility. Power tends to corrupt and absolute power corrupts absolutely. Great men are almost always bad men, even when they exercise influence and not authority: still more when you superadd the tendency or the certainty of corruption by authority. There is no

worse heresy than that the office sanctifies the holder of it. That is the point at which the negation of Catholicism and the negation of Liberalism meet and keep high festival, and the end learns to justify the means. You would hang a man of no position, like Ravaillac; but if what one hears is true, then Elizabeth asked the gaoler to murder Mary, and William III ordered his Scots minister to extirpate a clan. Here are the greater names coupled with the greater crimes. You would spare these criminals, for some mysterious reason. I would hang them, higher than Haman, for reasons of quite obvious justice; still more, still higher, for the sake of historical science."

This exchange between Lord Acton and Bishop Creighton, who was also a British historian, was in the context of how it was the obligation of historians to hold those in authority accountable for the treatment of those deemed *dissidents* or *heretics*. It highlights the disparity between commoner and noble, and even Pope, simply because of their station in life.

Should we turn a blind eye to corruption and criminal behavior because it is committed by someone with power and position?

In his third letter to Creighton, Acton references a conversation with Anti-Corn Law League leader John Bright, who stated to him that *"If the people knew what sort of men statesmen were, they would rise and hang the whole lot of them."*

This sentiment reminds me of Paul's letter to Titus in which he says, *"An elder must be blameless, faithful to his wife, a man whose children believe and are not open to the charge of being wild and disobedient. Since an overseer manages God's household, he must be blameless—not overbearing, not quick-tempered, not given to drunkenness, not violent, not pursuing dishonest gain."* **Titus 1: 6-7** (NIV)

While this is directed toward appointing church leaders, we can make an argument that, since the entirety of Earth is God's creation, these are sound principals for electing our governmental leaders.

There is an old joke that says, *"The real reason that we can't have the Ten Commandments in a courthouse is because you cannot post, 'Thou shalt not steal, Thou shalt not commit adultery, and Thou shalt not lie,' in a building full of lawyers, judges, and politicians. It creates a hostile work environment."* But comedy is often the vehicle for unspoken truths.

During my career with the NYPD, I spent five years assigned to the Intelligence Division. Part of my assignment was providing dignitary protection to visitors to New York City. I have stood next to the famous and infamous from around the globe, including presidents, prime ministers, royalty, and the Pope.

Providing protection is a fine balancing act. You need to be close to the protectee, but *unseen*. You become part of the background. At the same time you are privy to a lot of information on the person behind the public façade. The United States Secret Service has a saying, *'Worthy of Trust and Confidence,'* and that is something you take to heart. Rarely will someone speak about what they saw or heard, because it endangers the protection mission. Like it or not, there is a symbiotic relationship that exists between the protector and protectee. I will admit that I served on several details guarding people I personally disliked, but you never allowed the personal to interfere with the professional.

I can tell you that the public face of many politicians and celebrities is diametrically opposed to the private. What you see is the public persona, and that is scripted. I have been in rooms where supposedly bitter political *enemies* are drinking and laughing with one another. We elevate and vilify people not based on what we actually know about them, but what we are told.

This pandemic will eventually pass, but it will leave us with many questions. Will we wring our hands and disingenuously ask, *"Where was God?"* Or will we finally wake up and take a long hard look at the actual cause of these problems, *Humanity*?

I will close this chapter and leave you with a quote from Alexis de Tocqueville, the 19th century French statesman, historian, and social philosopher: *"I sought for the greatness and genius of*

America in her commodious harbors and her ample rivers – and it was not there . . . in her fertile fields and boundless forests and it was not there . . . in her rich mines and her vast world commerce – and it was not there . . . in her democratic Congress and her matchless Constitution – and it was not there. Not until I went into the churches of America and heard her pulpits aflame with righteousness did I understand the secret of her genius and power. America is great because she is good, and if America ever ceases to be good, she will cease to be great."

Perhaps if we all focused more on observing Jesus' command to love God and one another, and held our elected representatives to this same standard, we would no longer have to ask where God was, because He would be alive and well inside us.

CHAPTER TWELVE

(Lessons From Job)

You have probably heard the quote: 'He has the patience of Job,' but did you ever stop for a moment to consider what that statement means?

The story of Job isn't really about patience; it is about *trusting* in the Lord when everything around you is falling to pieces.

Chapter 11 was added to this book around the time of Easter, but this chapter is taking place right before the 19th anniversary of September 11th. I'd wanted to get this book re-released earlier, but I guess God had other plans and now I know why.

Several weeks ago my wife introduced me to the preaching of Pastor J.D. Farage of Calvary Chapel Kaneohe in Hawaii. He has done some amazing sermons on Bible prophecy, especially regarding the end times, and I would highly recommend that you look at some of his sermons that are on YouTube. But what struck me, especially as I reflect on the upcoming anniversary of 9/11, was his Bible study on Job. If you have never read the book of Job, I would encourage you to, as I won't do it justice in the space allotted for this book.

The basic premise of my book, Where Was God? centers on the question of how could a loving God allow such bad things to happen.

"There was a man in the land of Uz, whose name was Job; and that man was perfect and upright, and one that feared God, and eschewed evil. And there were born unto him seven sons and three daughters. His substance also was seven thousand sheep, and three thousand camels, and five hundred yoke of oxen, and five hundred she asses, and a very great household; so that this man was the greatest of all the men of the east." **Job 1:1-3** (KJV)

Right from the beginning, we are told that Job was an upright man and that he feared God. It's also interesting to note that it is believed that Job lived in pre-Mosaic times, making his sacrifices even more significant because they weren't required. He was literally *ahead of his time*. He was so righteous that he was making offerings to guide even before they were required.

So what is about to befall him makes little sense to us and there is a very good reason for that. Job's fate was not sealed on Earth, but in Heaven.

Job 1:7-11, "*And the LORD said unto Satan, Whence comest thou? Then Satan answered the LORD, and said, From going to and fro in the earth, and from walking up and down in it. And the LORD said unto Satan, Hast thou considered my servant Job, that there is none like him in the earth, a perfect and an upright man, one that feareth God, and escheweth evil? Then Satan answered the LORD, and said, Doth Job fear God for nought? Hast not thou made an hedge about him, and about his house, and about all that he hath on every side? thou hast blessed the work of his hands, and his substance is increased in the land. But put forth thine hand now, and touch all that he hath, and he will curse thee to thy face.*" (KJV)

And there it is.

To paraphrase, 'Sure Job loves you, but that's only because you gave him everything. Take it away and he will not only turn away from You, but he will curse you to Your face.'

And what does God do? He *allows* Job to be tested.

Job 1:12 – "*And the LORD said unto Satan, Behold, all that he hath is in thy power; only upon himself put not forth thine hand.*" (KJV)

Job 2:6 – "*And the LORD said unto Satan, Behold, he is in thine hand; but save his life.*" (KJV)

This is a significant piece of scripture, because it tells us something very important. Satan, for all the authority he believes he has here on Earth, still cannot act without God's permission. He is not omniscient, he is not omnipotent, and he is not omnipresent. Only God is. He *thinks* he knows what Job will do, but only God *knows*. It also tells us that Satan can do only as much as God allows him to and nothing more.

The book of Job is filled with an incredible amount of intricacies, and entire books have been devoted to examining, so I recommend you open your Bibles and really take this book to heart.

The fate that befalls Job is horrific. As a man of extreme wealth and standing, he loses everything. Interestingly, the only thing Satan does not do is afflict Job's ability to talk, because he needs him to be able to speak, in order to curse God.

- His ten children were killed

- All his livestock are lost

- His wife turns from him

- A painful and grotesque physical ailment leaves him lying in ash, unable to eat or sleep

- His friends condemn him and harshly rebuke him for alleged sins

In the end, Job is beside himself. His friends, for lack of a better word, mean well, but they place the blame for what has befallen him at Job's feet.

In **Job 4:7**, his friend, Eliphaz, says, *"Remember, I pray thee, who ever perished, being innocent? or where were the righteous cut off?"* (KJV)

Hey, Job, if you had done nothing wrong, none of this would happen to you.

In **Job 8:6**, his friend Bildad says, *"If thou wert pure and upright; surely now He would awake for thee, and make the habitation of thy righteousness prosperous."* (KJV)

Job, if you had not done anything wrong, He would be there for you.

And last, but not least, his friend Zophar chimes.

Job 11:6, *"Know therefore that God exacteth of thee less than thine iniquity deserveth."* (KJV)

Think about this, Job, as bad as you are feeling, it's only a fraction of what you really deserve!

And what is Job's response to all of this? Remember, he knows that he has done nothing wrong to deserve the fate that has befallen him. In **Job 13:15**, he replies: *"Though He slay me, yet will I trust in Him."* (KJV)

Job does not understand why he is going through this horrific period, but he still puts his complete faith in God. His friends, absent any evidence, still accuse him; because they are caught up in their misguided belief that God would only permit this to happen to Job if he had sinned.

Job 16:2, *"I have heard many such things: miserable comforters are ye all."* (KJV)

Ever wonder where the saying, *with friends like this, who needs enemies,* came from? Wonder no more.

The engagement continues.

Now, to be fair, I think their rebuke wasn't done with malice, but out of pure ignorance; not that it makes it right. Job's plight is horrendous, but his friends make matters worse when they condemn him for doing things they cannot know, while he knows that he has not done them.

Think about this for a moment. There are forty-two chapters in the Book of Job, his friends show up toward the end of Chapter 2. That means for twenty-nine chapters, Job is sparring with his friends and it is not a simple argument. These friends are emphatically making the case that Job has aggrieved God with some heinous crime, which is why this judgement, including the deaths of his children, has been brought down against him. I mean, this conversation is about as confrontational as you can get without becoming physical.

Job 19:2-3, *"How long will ye vex my soul, and break me in pieces with words? These ten times have ye reproached me: ye are not ashamed that ye make yourselves strange to me."* (KJV)

Now remember, these are Job's friends. As bad as his situation was, these were the only three that showed up for him and now that friendship is on the verge of tatters. In fact, as bad as it is now, the verbal sparring continues through Chapter 31.

I remember thinking, the first time I read Job, that it was agonizingly long. Kids today use the acronym: TLDR which means, *Too Long; Didn't Read*. If anything fit this it would be these twenty-nine chapters. But now, as I read through them I realize that this argument is being told to us for a reason.

Job is the perfect book to explain the human condition. For twenty-nine chapters we witness humanity on display. From Job's wondering of why he is going through such affliction, to his questioning of God's righteousness in allowing such affliction to befall him. I mean, he is really experiencing a deeply profound crisis of faith, something I am sure many of us can relate to. Interestingly enough, something significant, but rarely mentioned, is that throughout the entirety of his suffering, which was not only extensive, but prolonged, Job never asks for God to heal him or return what he has lost, his children, his wealth, or his friendships. What he yearns for is the restoration of his relationship with God, basically echoing what Jesus said on the cross: *'Eli, Eli, lama sabachthani? that is to say, My God, my God, why hast thou forsaken me?'* **Matthew 27:46** (KJV)

We also see, through the lens of his *friends*, just how much we don't understand God and try to impart our knowledge on His actions. Instead of being comforters, we are often accusers. It's the old, 'Good things happen to good people and bad things happen to bad people,' philosophy. The spiritually immature mindset of Eliphaz, Bildad, and Zophar, would not allow them to realize that God's ways differ from ours. Their theology was along the lines of, 'Hey, Job, if God is doing this to you, then you must be bad.' If they didn't accuse Job of being sinful, then they would have to accept that God could do the same thing to them and they were not about to go down that road.

Job argues this point, in **Chapter 21:7-9**, *"Why do the wicked live on, growing old and increasing in power? They see their children established around them, their offspring before their eyes. Their homes are safe and free from fear; the rod of God is not on them."* (KJV)

In essence, he is chastising his friends: You claim God is punishing me, because I am wicked and have sinned, but don't the sinful prosper?

And if you think this is bad, just wait, because in **Chapter 32**, we are introduced to another antagonist, *Elihu son of Barakel the Buzite*, who is more than a bit miffed.

Job 32:4, *"Now Elihu had waited before speaking to Job because they were older than he. But when he saw that the three men had nothing more to say, his anger was aroused."* (NIV)

This is where things take a bit of a turn.

Until this point, two separate and distinct dialogues have been taking place: Job has been arguing, with little success, that he is without sin, and wondering why God has allowed this affliction to befall him, while his friends argue that God is just and would not be allowing this unless there was some *hidden* sin in Job's life.

Elihu's commentary lasts for a full six chapters. When he is finished, he is gone, but in these chapters he establishes several key points:

- He is angry with Job because Job sought to justify himself, rather than God. **Job 32:2**

- He is angry with the three friends, because they sought to condemn Job, even though they had no evidence to support their claims. **Job 32:3**

- He states unequivocally that *"It is unthinkable that God would do wrong, that the Almighty would pervert justice."* **Job 34:12** (NIV)

- He establishes God's sovereignty in that He sees everything, all the time: "*God has no need to examine people further, that they should come before him for judgment.*" **Job 34:23** (NIV)

- Whoever Elihu is, he is not for Job or his friends, but for God. "*The Almighty is beyond our reach and exalted in power; in his justice and great righteousness, he does not oppress.*" **Job 37:23** (NIV)

It is interesting that at no point is he interrupted. Job fought back against the accusations of Eliphaz, Bildad, and Zophar, as did they against him. But each of the four is silent during Elihu's rebuke of them, even though he is junior to them in age, which speaks to the truth of his words. It reminds me of **Matthew 11:25**, "*At that time Jesus answered and said, I thank thee, O Father, Lord of heaven and earth, because thou hast hid these things from the wise and prudent, and hast revealed them unto babes.*" (KJV)

I should note that some have argued that Elihu does not differ from the other three friends, contending that he also claims that Job has sinned, but there is something subtle that is often overlooked. Eliphaz, Bildad, and Zophar accuse Job of sinning against God *before* he suffered; Elihu tells Job that he sinned *after* he became afflicted by questioning God.

Job 36:22-23, "*God is exalted in his power. Who is a teacher like him? Who has prescribed his ways for him, or said to him, 'You have done wrong'?*" (NIV)

However, none of the men are prepared for what will happen next.

Job 38:1 – "*Then the LORD answered Job out of the whirlwind, and said, Who is this that darkeneth counsel by words without knowledge? Gird up now thy loins like a man; for I will demand of thee, and answer thou me. Where wast thou when I laid the foundations of the earth? declare, if thou hast understanding.*" (KJV)

Let's pause for a minute and take a moment to appreciate the gravity of the situation: **God is here**.

One minute the four men are hurling accusations and the next minute they are dumbstruck. Everything up till this point reminds me of four kids in their bedrooms, jumping on their beds, yelling at each other and just raising a ruckus. Then the bedroom door opens up and dad is standing there: Game over.

'Who do you think you are, that you can speak for Me? Where you there when I created everything? Speak now if your knowledge is equal to Mine!'

From the beginning, God puts all four of them in their place. Notice that God does not mention Elihu, nor does he rebuke his words. On a side note, there seems to be a prophetic connection between Elihu and Elijah in the Book of Malachi, the last book of the Old Testament.

"You have spoken arrogantly against me," says the LORD.... *"See, I will send the prophet Elijah to you before that great and dreadful day of the LORD comes."* **Malachi 3:13, 4:5** (NIV)

In **Job 40:2**, God first turns his attention toward Job, saying, *"Shall he that contendeth with the Almighty instruct him? he that reproveth God, let him answer it."* (KJV)

In essence, God is saying to Job: 'Do you have a problem with Me? Do you think you are My equal? Let's hear it.'

At this very moment, Job knows he is in way over his head. For twenty-nine chapters he went toe-to-toe against his *friend's* accusations, but right now he is in the presence of the Almighty and staring at the ground wishing he could disappear.

In verses 3-5, Job answers, saying, *"Behold, I am vile; what shall I answer thee? I will lay mine hand upon my mouth. Once have I spoken; but I will not answer: yea, twice; but I will proceed no further."* (KJV)

How many times have we found ourselves going through a trial, crying out to the Lord, and questioning Him on why he is letting it happen to us? I'm ashamed to admit it, but I know I have. Now imagine the skies open up and a voice booms out. Talk about a wake-up call! It's one thing to *think* about how great God is, but it's a completely different thing to *see* the awesome majesty of God.

It reminds me of something a friend once said to me, when we were discussing salvation. He said, "Well when I get to Heaven I'm just going to have a talk with God."

Really?

You're just going to pull up a chair in the throne room and think you're going to have a fireside chat with the Almighty on why you belong there? I think you might be overstating your abilities a bit.

But God's not done reminding Job of just who He is.

Verse 8: *"Wilt thou also disannul my judgment? wilt thou condemn me, that thou mayest be righteous?"* (KJV)

Job had not only sought to contend with God, he'd also accused God of unrighteousness; in essence, the creation questioning the Creator. So God backs him into the proverbial corner and says, in verses 10-14: *"Deck thyself now with majesty and excellency; and array thyself with glory and beauty. Cast abroad the rage of thy wrath: and behold every one that is proud, and abase him. Look on every one that is proud, and bring him low; and tread down the wicked in their place. Hide them in the dust together; and bind their faces in secret. Then will I also confess unto thee that thine own right hand can save thee."* (KJV)

'You think you are like Me, Job? Well, then raise yourself up in your glory and assume the rule of the world; when you can do these things, get back to Me.'

Job 38-41 is about God establishing who He is, the Creator of all things. And who we are? His creations.

Sometimes, like Job, we forget our place. Why do things happen? Well, they often happen because of us, and sometimes they happen for reasons unknown to us, at least in our limited knowledge, but they can't and don't happen outside God's will for us.

In **Revelation 3:7**, Jesus says, "*And to the angel of the church in Philadelphia write, 'These things says He who is holy, He who is true, "He who has the key of David, He who opens and no one shuts, and shuts and no one opens."* (KJV)

God reminds us He alone is the Almighty. He alone knows all things.

God has not only spoken *to* Job, but he is about to speak *about* Job. In verse 8, He says to Job's friends, "*Ye have not spoken of me the thing which is right, like my servant Job.*" (KJV)

And what happens when God speaks to the others? Well, it's going to cost them dearly.

Job 42:8, "*So now take seven bulls and seven rams and go to my servant Job and sacrifice a burnt offering for yourselves. My servant Job will pray for you, and I will accept his prayer and not deal with you according to your folly.*" (NIV)

This was not a minor penalty, this was going to hurt. To understand, you need to recognize the importance of livestock in the days of Job. They were a sign of wealth and standing; besides providing food, clothing, transportation, and fuel.

In Chapter 42, Job stops whining and humbles himself before God. Then, and this is really important, despite everything that his friends unjustly accused him of, he *prayed* for them.

What? After all the vile and unjust accusatory things they said about him? Yep.

After Job prays for his friends, God releases him from his ordeal. God rewards his loyal servant, who remained true to Him, as He knew he would, and returned twofold everything that had been taken away.

Will we ever be able to make sense, this side of Heaven, of man's inhumanity to man? I don't think so. Our knowledge is just too limited to fathom the scope of such depravity, but I take solace in knowing that God understands it all. I also trust in His wisdom and righteousness.

As it says in **Isaiah 55:11** – *"So is my word that goes out from my mouth: It will not return to me empty, but will accomplish what I desire and achieve the purpose for which I sent it."* (NIV)

Nothing on Earth occurs without God's consent and if we cannot understand it, that is because we are not Him and, to me, that is a blessing. But we must always remember the lessons of Job and, when we find ourselves struggling and suffering, give Him praise. This life is but a vapor, but we have been given the gift of eternal life through the death and resurrection of our Lord and Savior, Jesus Christ.

SINNER'S PRAYER

I am not a preacher, nor am I a formally educated theologian. What I am is a Christian who has been saved by the grace of God and I am using the ability He gave me to write, so I can reach out to others. If this book saves only *one person*, then it was worth everything I went through that day, and continue to go through, to bring you this message of salvation.

During my life, I have encountered many people who believe that they are unworthy; they believe that they have sinned too greatly for God to ever love or forgive them. To them I say you're wrong.

The truth is, on our own, there is nothing we can do to get into Heaven. That is why salvation is a gift. No matter your sin, God can wash it away and all it takes is something as easy as the *A, B, C*'s.

Admit that you are a sinner - *"For all have sinned, and come short of the glory of God."* **Romans 3:23** (KJV)

Believe that Jesus died for your sins, rose from the dead, and paid the price for your sin in full - *"Believe on the Lord Jesus Christ, and thou shalt be saved."* **Acts 16:31** (KJV)

Confess your sins - *"If we confess our sins, he is faithful and just to forgive us our sins, and to cleanse us from all unrighteousness."* **1 John 1:9** (KJV)

It's not about what you do, it's about what God does.

If that is you, and you've never trusted in Jesus before, then I encourage you to recite the *Sinner's Prayer* and begin your relationship with God today.

Dear Lord Jesus, I know that I am a sinner, and I ask for Your forgiveness.

I believe You died for my sins and rose from the dead. I turn from my sins and ask that You come into my heart and life.

I want to trust in you and develop a personal relationship with You, as my Lord and Savior.

In Your Name. Amen.

IN MEMORIAM

(The Lost)

"All Gave Some, Some Gave All."

The terror attack of September 11th, 2001, marked the single deadliest day for the NYPD in its long and storied history. When the dust finally settled, the death toll for the members of the New York City Police Department numbered twenty-three, but what we didn't know then was that it was just the beginning. In less than two years the realization would finally set-in, as we lost more officers who became sick from the toxins they ingested that day.

In the proceeding years, the number of NYPD officers who have become sick and have died from 9/11 related illnesses' has continued to skyrocket. This is equally true for the members of the FDNY and Port Authority Police Department, as well as the wider community of 9/11 workers and victims. The last estimate I have heard was that we lose an average of one person every 2.7 days.

To properly list the names of everyone who has died, because of that horrific attack, would require an entire book of its own and I am not the person to do that.

On the following pages is a list of the members of the NYPD who died during and after the attack. They are the epitome of the NYPD motto: *Fidelis Ad Mortem.*

Sadly, this list will only continue to grow with each passing day. But as long as I am around, I will continually update this list, because I believe it is part of my solemn obligation to never forget their heroism and sacrifice.

DIED IN THE 9/11 ATTACK

Sergeant John G. Coughlin
Sergeant Michael S. Curtin
Sergeant Rodney C. Gillis
Sergeant Timothy A. Roy, Sr.

Detective Claude D. Richards
Detective Joseph V. Vigiano

Police Officer John D'Allara
Police Officer Vincent G. Danz
Police Officer Mark J. Ellis
Police Officer Robert Fazio
Police Officer Jerome Dominguez
Police Officer Stephen P. Driscoll
Police Officer Ronald P. Kloepfer
Police Officer Thomas M. Langone
Police Officer James P. Leahy
Police Officer Brian G. McDonnell
Police Officer John W. Perry
Police Officer Glen K. Pettit
Police Officer Moira A. Reddy-Smith
Police Officer Ramon Suarez
Police Officer Paul Talty
Police Officer Santos Valentin, Jr.
Police Officer Walter E. Weaver

DIED FROM 9/11 EXPOSURE

Chief of Detectives William Allee

Assistant Deputy Commissioner Thomas P. Doepfner

Assistant Chief Michael V. Quinn

Deputy Chief Steven J. Bonano
Deputy Chief Vincent A. DeMarino
Deputy Chief James G. Molloy

Inspector Donald G. Feser
Inspector James Guida
Inspector Richard D. Winter

Captain Carmine C. Cantalino
Captain Barry Galfano
Captain Edward C. Gilpin
Captain Edward J. McGreal
Captain Dennis Morales
Captain Ronald G. Peifer, Sr.
Captain Peter L. Pischera
Captain Scott V. Stelmok

Lieutenant Rebecca A. Buck
Lieutenant Steven L. Cioffi
Lieutenant Jeffrey W. Francis
Lieutenant Luis A. Lopez
Lieutenant Jacqueline McCarthy
Lieutenant Jennifer Meehan

Lieutenant Brian S. Mohamed

Lieutenant Paul Murphy

Lieutenant Carlos J. Ocasio

Lieutenant Phillip E. Panzarella

Lieutenant Christopher M. Pupo

Lieutenant Gerald Rex

Lieutenant Robert Rice

Lieutenant Kenneth W. Rosello

Lieutenant John Charles Rowland

Lieutenant James D. Russell

Lieutenant James E. Ryan

Lieutenant Marci Simms

Lieutenant William H. Wanser, III

Sergeant Alex W. Baez

Sergeant Gerard T. Beyrodt

Sergeant Patrick J. Boyle

Sergeant Christopher M. Christodoulou

Sergeant Charles J. Clark

Sergeant Patrick T. Coyne

Sergeant Garrett S. Danza

Sergeant Paul M. Ferrara

Sergeant Gary M. Franklin

Sergeant Michael J. Galvin

Sergeant Charles R. Gunzelman

Sergeant Claire T. Hanrahan

Sergeant Michael V. Incontrera

Sergeant Wayne A. Jackson

Sergeant Scott Johnston

Sergeant Mark Lawler

Sergeant Robert P. Masci

Sergeant Colleen A. McGowan

Sergeant Michael J. McHugh

Sergeant Patrick P. Murphy

Sergeant Edmund P. Murray

Sergeant Anthony Napolitano

Sergeant Terrence S. O'Hara

Sergeant Donald J. O'Leary, Jr.

Sergeant Louis R. Pioli

Sergeant Michael W. Ryan

Sergeant Stephen P. Scalza

Sergeant Jacqueline C. Schaefer

Sergeant Harold J. Smith

Sergeant Barbara A. Sullivan

Sergeant Edward D. Thompson

Sergeant Michael B. Wagner

Detective Sandra Y. Adrian

Detective I Gerard A. Ahearn

Detective James J. Albanese

Detective Sixto Almonte

Detective Luis G. Alvarez

Detective Thomas J. Barnitt

Detective Aslyn A. Beckles

Detective Joseph A. Cavitolo

Detective Christopher Cranston

Detective Angel A. Creagh

Detective Traci L. Tack-Czajkowski

Detective Kevin A. Czartoryski

Detective Annetta G. Daniels

Detective Michael K. Davis

Detective Corey J. Diaz

Detective Leroy Dixon

Detective Pedro Esponda, Jr.

Detective Luis G. Fernandez

Detective Carmen M. Figueroa

Detective Stuart F. Fishkin

Detective Sean P. Franklin

Detective James T. Giery

Detective Charles G. Gittens, Jr.

Detective Michael E. Glazer

Detective John E. Goggin

Detective Kevin G. Hawkins

Detective Michael R. Henry

Detective Alick W. Herrmann

Detective William J. Holfester

Detective Nathaniel Holland, Jr.

Detective Steven Hom

Detective Charles J. Humphry

Detective William D. Kinane

Detective John F. Kristoffersen

Detective Stephen T. Kubinski

Detective Robert F. Larke

Detective Michael L. Ledek

Detective Jeffrey A. Lee

Detective Christian R. Lindsay

Detective Thomas J. Lyons

Detective John J. Marshall

Detective Tommy L. Merriweather

Detective Mark Mkwanazi

Detective James W. Monahan

Detective Robert A. Montanez

Detective Michael P. Morales

Detective John K. Muller

Detective Maureen M. O'Flaherty

Detective Edwin Ortiz

Detective Joseph Paolillo

Detective Philip T. Perry

Detective Joseph L. Pidoto

Detective Andrea R. Rainer

Detective George C. Remouns, Jr.

Detective Ronald A. Richards

Detective Roberto L. Rivera

Detective Joseph M. Roman

Detective John A. Russo

Detective Thomas Santoro

Detective James A. Schiavone, Jr.

Detective Joseph E. Seabrook

Detective Basilio A. Simons

Detective Andrew L. Siroka

Detective Christopher Strucker

Detective Sally A. Thompson

Detective William B. Titus, Jr.

Detective Harry Valentin

Detective Dennis J. Vickery

Detective Thomas P. Ward

Detective Thomas F. Weiner, Jr.

Detective Richard H. Wentz

Detective Megan K. Carr-Wilks

Detective Jennifer A. Williams

Detective Robert W. Williamson

Detective John T. Young

Detective James Zadroga

Police Officer Curtis J. Bako

Police Officer Karen E. Barnes

Police Officer Judy Ann Ghany-Barounis

Police Officer Ronald G. Becker, Jr.

Police Officer James A. Betso

Police Officer Derrick Bishop

Police Officer Scott Blackshaw

Police Officer Marie Ann Patterson-Bohanan

Police Officer Frank M. Bolusi

Police Officer Thomas G. Brophy

Police Officer James M. Burke

Police Officer Audrey P. Capra

Police Officer Madeline Carlo

Police Officer Yolanda Cawley

Police Officer Peter D. Ciaccio

Police Officer Daniel C. Conroy

Police Officer Anthony D'Erasmo

Police Officer Anthony DeJesus

Police Officer Michael O. Diamond

Police Officer Kenneth X. Domenech

Police Officer Renee Dunbar

Police Officer Robert M. Ehmer

Police Officer Otto R. Espinoza

Police Officer William P. Farley

Police Officer Keith A. Ferrara

Police Officer John P. Ferrari

Police Officer Edward M. Ferraro

Police Officer Alexander Figueroa

Police Officer Nicholas G. Finelli

Police Officer Edward J. Fitzgerald

Police Officer Scott N. Gaines

Police Officer Thomas J. Gallagher

Police Officer Matthew J. Gay

Police Officer Anthony C. Giambra, Jr.

Police Officer James J. Godbee

Police Officer Robert C. Grossman

Police Officer Dave E. Guevara

Police Officer Diane F. Halbran

Police Officer Michael Hance

Police Officer Anthony Hanlon

Police Officer Raymond Harris

Police Officer Joseph F. Heid

Police Officer Robert B. Helmke

Police Officer Richard G. Holland

Police Officer Demetrias Hopkins

Police Officer Richard Jakubowsky

Police Officer Deborah A. Garbutt-Jeff

Police Officer Cheryl D. Johnson

Police Officer Paul J. Johnson

Police Officer Louise M. Johnston

Police Officer Robert W. Kaminski

Police Officer Charles M. Karen

Police Officer William J. King

Police Officer Gary L. Koch

Police Officer Kelly C. Korchak

Police Officer Fred J. Krines

Police Officer Andrew J. Lewis

Police Officer Richard Lopez

Police Officer Frank G. Macri

Police Officer David Mahmoud

Police Officer Shaun M. Mahoney

Police Officer Vito S. Mauro

Police Officer Gary G. Mausberg

Police Officer Patrick T. McGovern

Police Officer Denis R. McLarney

Police Officer Christopher S. McMurry

Police Officer Gregory V. Melita

Police Officer Mark J. Natale

Police Officer Robert J. Nicosia

Police Officer Jason H. Offner

Police Officer Robert Ortiz

Police Officer Robert V. Oswain, Jr.

Police Officer Patrice M. Ott

Police Officer Allison M. Palmer

Police Officer Angelo Peluso, Jr.

Police Officer Francis T. Pitone

Police Officer Joseph C. Pagnani

Police Officer William G. Parker

Police Officer Frank J. Pizzo

Police Officer Christine A. Reilly

Police Officer Lawrence J. Rivera

Police Officer Peter O. Rodriguez

Police Officer Matthew S. von Seydewitz

Police Officer Peter M. Sheridan, Jr.

Police Officer Robert S. Summers

Police Officer Richard E. Taylor

Police Officer Martin Tom

Police Officer Reginald Umpthery, Sr.

Police Officer Manuel Vargas, Jr.

Police Officer Perry T. Villani

Police Officer John F. Vierling, Jr.

Police Officer William T. Walsh

Police Officer Ronald E. Weintraub

Police Officer Wade J. Williams

Police Officer Kenneth W. Wolf

Police Officer George Mon Cheng Wong

Police Officer Robert A. Zane, Jr.

Auto Mechanic Elmis A. Fisher

(As of: April 22, 2020 – Source: NYPD, ODMP)

SUPPORT

(The 9/11 Community)

I attribute my ability to tell stories as being a gift from God. While I wrote this book from my heart, I also believe God divinely inspired it and as because of this I deserve no credit. I will also take no royalties from the sale of this book, because to me this is God's money.

From the beginning, every cent that has been raised from the sale of this book has been donated. To maintain complete transparency, I have posted all the donations and the organizations who received them.

In the past I had used this platform to recommend charities to contribute to, but as I look around I realize that there are so many worthwhile causes within our own circle that we should support. This is especially true when we realize that so many are struggling during these uncertain financial times. Seek God's guidance first and he will lead you.

Thank you & God Bless.

THE W.T.C. CROSS

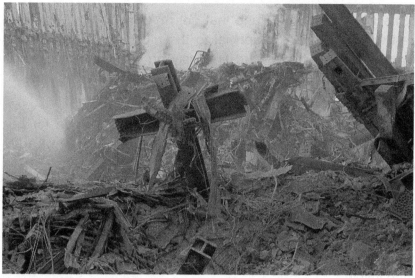

Photo courtesy of Anne Bybee-Williams © 2001
(abybee1@gmail.com)

This is the iconic photo taken at Ground Zero, by Anne Bybee, following the attacks of September 11th, 2001.

Bybee was part of the National Disaster Medical System (NDMS) Mission Support Team, which provided help to the Disaster Medical Assistance Teams (DMAT), at Ground Zero.

After a few days she found herself numb and a sense of hopelessness set in, as she stared up at the massive pile of rubble, the remains of the World Trade Center, which had been the focal point of the New York City skyline only days earlier.

Then one day she saw it - a Cross.

"As I was staring at that, I got a sense of peace," Bybee said. "I got a very strong message. That message was, 'You are not alone. I am here.'"

The longer she looked at it, the more she was moved. To her the other material wrapped around it resembled the remnants of the clothes that Jesus would have worn.

She was not the only one that got that message. The Cross came to mean something special to the multitude of rescue and recovery workers who worked tirelessly on what became known as *The Pile*. It provided a sense of comfort during this time of tragedy, a reminder they were not alone.

I am honored and extremely thankful to Ms. Bybee for her permission in using this photo for the cover, as I believe it truly conveys the spirit of this book.

For those who have asked, "Where Was God?" The answer is, "Where He always is, with us."

We are the ones who are lost and need to find our way back to Him, but if we look closely, we will see all the signs we need to follow.

ABOUT THE AUTHOR

Andrew Nelson spent twenty-two years in law enforcement, including twenty years with the New York City Police Department. During his tenure with the NYPD he served as a detective in the elite Intelligence Division, conducting investigations and providing dignitary protection to many world leaders. He achieved the rank of sergeant before retiring in 2005.

He is the author of both the James Maguire and Alex Taylor mystery series, and the NYPD Cold Case novella series. He has also written several non-fiction books including: *Where Was God? An NYPD first responder's search for answers following the terror attack of September 11th 2001*, and two which chronicle the insignia of the New York City Police Department's Emergency Service Unit

For more information please visit us at:

www.andrewgnelson.org

ANDREW G.
NELSON

Made in the USA
Middletown, DE
31 July 2021